A journey of healing through universal guidance

Evolution through
Grief, Anxiety & Depression

Written by
SAMIR MISHRA

BLUEROSE PUBLISHERS
India | U.K.

Copyright © Samir Mishra 2024

All rights reserved by author. No part of this publication may be reproduced, stored in a retrieval system or transmitted in any form or by any means, electronic, mechanical, photocopying, recording or otherwise, without the prior permission of the author. Although every precaution has been taken to verify the accuracy of the information contained herein, the publisher assume no responsibility for any errors or omissions. No liability is assumed for damages that may result from the use of information contained within.

BlueRose Publishers takes no responsibility for any damages, losses, or liabilities that may arise from the use or misuse of the information, products, or services provided in this publication.

For permissions requests or inquiries regarding this publication, please contact:

BLUEROSE PUBLISHERS
www.BlueRoseONE.com
info@bluerosepublishers.com
+91 8882 898 898
+4407342408967

ISBN: 978-93-6452-146-8

Cover design: Tahira
Typesetting: Tanya Raj Upadhyay

First Edition: August 2024

Introduction

Life is an intricate tapestry woven with threads of joy, sorrow, triumph, and struggle. Among the most challenging threads to navigate are those of grief, anxiety, and depression. These emotional states, though deeply personal, are universal in their capacity to touch us all. They can arise from a myriad of experiences—loss of a loved one, personal failures, traumatic events, or even seemingly inexplicable sources. Yet, despite their ubiquity, they often leave us feeling isolated, misunderstood, and overwhelmed.

This book seeks to shed light on these profound aspects of the human condition, offering a comprehensive exploration of how they manifest and affect our lives. Through an examination of both scientific insights and personal narratives, it delves into the biological, psychological, and social dimensions of these emotions. The author's aim is not only to understand their origins and impacts but also to provide practical strategies for coping and healing.

Each chapter is designed to guide you through the complexities of these emotional states, offering tools and perspectives to help you navigate your own experiences. Whether you are grappling with the fresh wound of a recent loss, the relentless grip of anxiety, or the heavy weight of depression, this book offers a ray of hope. It emphasizes the importance of self-compassion, the value of seeking professional help, and the power of community support.

By sharing stories of those who have walked similar paths and emerged stronger, this book aims to inspire resilience and foster a sense of connection. It underscores the idea that while these experiences are undeniably painful, they also hold the potential for profound personal growth and transformation. In facing and understanding these emotions, we can learn to manage them more effectively and find a way to move forward with renewed strength and clarity.

This book is an invitation to explore, understand, and ultimately transform the way we deal with grief, anxiety, and depression. Through this exploration, may you find the tools and insights needed to navigate your own emotional landscape with greater ease and resilience.

Table of Contents

Introduction .... *iii*

Chapter 1: Understanding Grief *1*

Chapter 2: Exploring Anxiety *12*

Chapter 3: The Depths of Depression *23*

Chapter 4: Universal Guidance *34*

Chapter 5: Karmic Balance *45*

Chapter 6: Spiritual Healing *56*

Chapter 7: Self-Healing Practices *67*

Chapter 8: The Earthly Journey *78*

Chapter 9: Energy Connections *88*

Chapter 10: Aligning with Universal Truth *98*

Chapter 11: Dealing with Life Situations *109*

Chapter 12: Finding the Way Within *120*

Chapter 13: Taking the First Step *130*

Chapter 14: Becoming a Channel *141*

Chapter 1: Understanding Grief

The Nature of Grief

Grief is an emotion that profoundly shapes the human experience. It is a universal yet deeply personal response to loss, manifesting in myriad ways that rejects a one-size-fits-all explanation. The experience of grief can feel like an uncharted territory where familiar landmarks are suddenly obscured, creating a landscape where one's emotional bearings are constantly shifting. It is in this disorienting space that individuals often find themselves grappling with a range of emotions that can be both bewildering and overwhelming.

The first encounter with grief often brings a sense of shock or disbelief. The mind struggles to accept the reality of the loss that has occurred. This initial stage can be marked by numbness, a protective mechanism that insulates the individual from the full impact of their sorrow. It's as if the psyche is giving itself time to prepare for the emotional storm that is to come.

As the reality of the loss begins to sink in, the emotional numbness may give way to a flood of feelings. Sadness, anger, guilt, and despair can intermingle in a chaotic dance, leaving the individual feeling unmoored. Each emotion demands attention, yet they often arrive in no particular order and vary in intensity. One moment might be consumed by tears, while the next is filled with a sense of emptiness or rage. This unpredictability can be one of the most challenging aspects of grieving, as it defies any attempt to impose order or predictability on the process.

Grief also has a way of reaching into the past, bringing back memories and regrets that may have lain dormant for years. The mind sifts through these remnants, sometimes finding solace in cherished moments and at other times becoming mired in thoughts of what might have been. This introspection can be both a source of comfort and a trigger for deeper sorrow, as it underscores the permanence of the loss.

The physical manifestations of grief are no less varied. It can disrupt sleep, appetite, and energy levels, leaving the body as weary as the mind. The heart may literally ache, and the weight of sorrow can feel like a tangible burden pressing down on the chest. These symptoms are a reminder that grief is not confined to the realm of emotions but is an all-encompassing experience that affects the whole being.

Social interactions during this time can become difficult. Well-meaning friends and family members may offer comfort or advice that, however kindly intended, can feel hollow or even hurtful. A grieving person may find themselves withdrawing, seeking solace in solitude where they can process their emotions without the added pressure of social expectations. Yet, there can also be moments of profound connection, where a shared memory or a simple gesture of kindness provides a flicker of light in the darkness.

Grief is not a linear process with a clear endpoint. It ebbs and flows, sometimes receding into the background only to surge forward unexpectedly. Over time, the intensity of the emotions may diminish, but the absence of the loved one remains a constant presence. The challenge lies in finding a way to live with that absence, to integrate the loss into the fabric of one's life without allowing it to define every moment.

Understanding the nature of grief is an ongoing endeavor, one that requires patience, self-compassion, and a willingness to confront the depths of one's own emotions. It is a testament to the strength of the human spirit that, even in the face of profound loss, there remains a capacity for healing and for finding meaning amidst the sorrow.

Personal Experiences

Grief, anxiety, and depression have touched my life in ways that are both profound and deeply personal. I remember the first time I encountered the weight of grief. It was the loss of a beloved family member, someone who had been a constant presence in my life. The initial shock was numbing, as if my mind was trying to protect me from the full impact. The days that followed were a blur, filled with a sense of non-acceptance for that reality which I was a witness to. . I found myself going through the motions, surrounded by people who were similarly lost in their own sorrow.

The anxiety that accompanied this grief was a new and unwelcome visitor. It manifested in ways I had not anticipated. Simple tasks became monumental challenges. I would find myself paralyzed by the fear of making a mistake or disappointing others. The anxiety was insidious, creeping into every aspect of my life. It was not just the fear of the unknown, but a pervasive sense of dread that seemed to have no specific cause. Nights were the hardest, as my mind would race with endless what-ifs, leaving me exhausted and yet unable to sleep.

Depression soon followed, casting a long shadow over my days. It was not just sadness, but a profound sense of emptiness. Activities that once brought joy felt meaningless. I withdrew from friends and family, isolating myself in despair. The world seemed to move on without me, and I felt like a spectator in my own life. It was as if I was trapped in a fog, unable to see a way out.

During this time, I sought solace in various ways. I turned to writing as a means of processing my emotions. Writing allowed me to express what I could not say out loud. It was a form of therapy, a way to make sense of the chaos in my mind. I also found comfort in nature, taking long walks in the park. The simple act of being outside, surrounded by the beauty of the natural world, provided a brief respite from the turmoil within.

Support from others was crucial. I learned the importance of reaching out, even when it felt like the hardest thing to do. Conversations with friends, family, and counselors helped to lift some of the burden. They offered perspectives that I had not considered and reminded me that I was not alone. There were moments of connection that brought light into the darkness, however fleeting they might have been.

Reflecting on these experiences, I have come to understand that dealing with grief, anxiety, and depression is not a defined process but incorporate ways to un-layer them, bit by bit, through efforts which gradually lead us to an understanding that life situations can be more than difficult but can be healed and embraced. There are good days and bad days; moments of clarity and times of confusion as inherent aspects of life situations which are constantly presented before us to deal with. It is for us to acknowledge that healing is not a destination but a journey of small steps. Each step, no matter how small, is a testament to resilience. It is about finding the strength to keep moving forward, even when the path is uncertain.

These personal experiences have shaped me into who I am today. They have taught me about the depths of human emotion and the capacity for recovery. While the scars remain, they are a reminder of the battles fought and the progress made. It is a journey marked by challenges, but also by growth and self-discovery.

Grief in Different Cultures

In the tapestry of human experience, grief is a universal thread, yet its expression is as varied as the cultures that weave it. Each society has its own beliefs, and customs that shape the way people mourn, creating a rich mosaic of mourning practices across the globe. This diversity provides a window into the collective psyche of different cultures, revealing how they cope with loss and find meaning in the face of death.

In some cultures, grief is a communal affair, with the entire community coming together to support the bereaved. For instance, in many African societies, mourning is a collective process where the community gathers to sing, dance, and share stories about the deceased. This collective mourning not only honors the life of the departed but also reinforces social bonds and provides emotional support to the grieving family. The communal aspect of grief in these cultures highlights the importance of social connections and the role of the community in the healing process.

Contrastingly, in many Western cultures, grief is often seen as a private, individual experience. The emphasis is on personal reflection and emotional expression, with rituals such as funerals and memorial services providing a space for individuals to process their loss. This individualistic approach to grief can be both a source of solace and a challenge. On one hand, it allows for a deeply personal and introspective mourning process. On the other, it can sometimes lead to feelings of isolation, as the burden of grief is borne largely alone.

In Japan, the practice of mourning is deeply influenced by Buddhist traditions. The concept of impermanence (mujō) is central to Buddhist teachings, and this belief permeates the grieving process. Funerals are elaborate affairs, with rituals designed to guide the deceased's spirit to the afterlife and provide comfort to the living. The Japanese approach to grief emphasizes acceptance of death as a natural part of life, encouraging mourners to find peace in the transient nature of existence.

In Mexico, the Day of the Dead (Día de los Muertos) is a vibrant celebration that honors deceased loved ones.

This tradition, which blends indigenous practices with Catholicism, involves creating altars (ofrendas) adorned with photos, mementos, and favorite foods of the departed. The belief is that the spirits of the dead return to visit their families during this time, and the living celebrate their lives with joy and remembrance. This festive approach to mourning underscores the enduring connection between the living and the dead, transforming grief into a celebration of life.

In the Islamic tradition, grief is expressed through a series of prescribed rituals that provide structure and support to the bereaved. The body is washed and shrouded, prayers are recited, and the community comes together to offer condolences and support. The emphasis is on submission to the will of God (Allah) and finding solace in faith. This structured approach to grief helps mourners navigate their loss within a framework of religious beliefs and communal support.

These cultural variations in grieving practices illustrate that while the pain of loss is a shared human experience, the ways in which we process and express that pain are deeply influenced by our cultural contexts. Understanding these differences not only broadens our perspective on grief but also fosters empathy and respect for the diverse ways in which people around the world honor their loved ones and cope with loss.

Grief and Time

Time has an uncanny way of altering our relationship with grief. In the immediate aftermath of loss, time seems to stretch, every minute weighted with the rawness of pain. The clock's tick is almost an attack, a reminder that life persists even as our world feels irreparably shattered. Conversations with friends and loved ones often revolve around platitudes like 'Time heals all wounds', but in the depths of grief, such words can feel hollow, even dismissive.

Initially, the days blend into an indistinguishable blur, each one a mirror of the other, filled with the same aching void. It's as if the loss has created a chasm in time itself, a rift that prevents us from moving forward. We find ourselves caught in the past, clinging to memories and moments that seem to be slipping through our fingers like sand. The future, once a vast landscape of possibilities, now feels uncertain and obscure. .

As time progresses, the acute pain may dull, but it often gives way to a more chronic, lingering sorrow. This phase is deceptive; the world expects us to have 'moved on', yet on the inside, we may still feel as though we are navigating a labyrinth of emotions. It's during this period that the complexity of grief becomes most apparent. The initial shock has worn off, but the sense of loss remains, woven into the fabric of our daily lives.

Our relationship with time during grief is not linear. There are moments when we may feel a semblance of normalcy, only to be blindsided by waves of sadness triggered by a song, a scent, or an anniversary. These triggers remind us that grief is cyclical, not something that can be neatly compartmentalized or scheduled. It ebbs and flows, often without warning, making it difficult to predict how we will feel from one day to the next.

This unpredictable nature of grief can exacerbate feelings of anxiety and depression. The uncertainty of not knowing when the next wave of sorrow will hit can be deeply unsettling. We may find ourselves bracing for impact, living in a state of heightened alertness that takes a toll on our mental and physical well-being. Sleep becomes elusive, appetite fluctuates, and the world can seem like a series of potential emotional landmines.

Yet, within this tumultuous experience, there are also moments of profound clarity. Time allows us to reflect, to understand the depth of our loss, and to recognize the enduring impact it has on our lives. These moments are not about finding closure but about integrating the loss into our ongoing narrative. We learn to coexist with our grief, to carry it with us rather than trying to leave it behind.

It's important to acknowledge that everyone's timeline of grief is unique. Some may find solace in rituals and routines, while others might need the freedom to explore their emotions without constraint. There is no right or wrong way to grieve, and the process is as individual as the relationships we mourn.

In the end, time does not heal all wounds in the conventional sense. Instead, it offers us the space to grow around our grief, to build a life that accommodates our loss rather than being defined by it. Through this process, we may discover resilience we never knew we had, and a deeper understanding of the human capacity for love and endurance.

Chapter 2: Exploring Anxiety

What is Anxiety?

Anxiety is a shadow that often lurks just beyond the periphery of our conscious minds, a persistent hum that vibrates through the fabric of our daily lives. To understand anxiety, one must delve into its multifaceted nature, recognizing it as both a mental and physiological experience that can vary greatly from one person to another.

At its core, anxiety is a natural human response to perceived threats or stressors. It is an evolutionary mechanism designed to keep us alert and prepared for potential dangers. In this sense, anxiety is not inherently negative; it has a purpose and can even be beneficial in certain situations. For example, the anxiety one might feel before a big presentation or an important exam can serve as a motivating force, pushing us to prepare thoroughly and perform at our best. However, when anxiety becomes chronic or overwhelming, it can have a debilitating effect on our lives.

The experience of anxiety is deeply personal and can manifest in a multitude of ways. For some, it may present as a constant state of worry or unease, a feeling of being perpetually on edge. Others might experience it more acutely, in the form of panic attacks or intense episodes of fear that seem to come out of nowhere. Physical symptoms often accompany these feelings, such as a racing heart, shortness of breath, sweating, or trembling. These symptoms can be particularly distressing, as they create a feedback loop where the physical sensations of anxiety amplify the emotional experience, and vice versa.

It is also important to recognize that anxiety does not exist in a vacuum. It is often intertwined with other emotional states, such as grief and depression. These emotions can feed into one another, creating a complex web that can be difficult to untangle. For instance, someone who is grieving the loss of a loved one might find themselves grappling with anxiety about the future or their ability to cope with the loss. Similarly, those who struggle with depression may experience heightened levels of anxiety, as their negative thoughts and feelings exacerbate their sense of dread and apprehension.

Understanding anxiety requires a compassionate and nuanced approach. It is not simply a matter of 'worrying too much' or being unable to 'calm down'.

Rather, it is a deeply ingrained response that can be influenced by a variety of factors, including genetics, past experiences, and current life circumstances. It is essential to acknowledge the individual nature of anxiety, as each person's experience is unique and shaped by their personal history and context.

Navigating the labyrinth of anxiety can be challenging, but it is not an insurmountable task. By fostering a deeper understanding of what anxiety is and how it manifests, we can begin to develop strategies to manage it effectively. This might involve seeking professional help, practicing mindfulness and relaxation techniques, or finding healthy ways to cope with stress. Ultimately, the goal is not to eliminate anxiety entirely, but to learn how to live with it in a way that allows us to lead fulfilling and meaningful lives.

Triggers of Anxiety

Anxiety often feels like an uninvited guest that arrives without warning, disrupting the delicate balance of our emotional state. The sources of this unwelcome intrusion are varied as they are pervasive, weaving through the fabric of our lives in ways both seen and unseen. The triggers that set off these waves of anxiety can be deeply personal, rooted in past experiences, or can stem from more immediate, tangible stressors in our everyday lives.

One of the most profound triggers is the experience of loss. Whether it's the death of a loved one, the end of a significant relationship, or even the loss of a job, these events can shake the foundation of our emotional well-being. The uncertainty that accompanies loss leaves us vulnerable, questioning our stability and our future. This vulnerability can manifest as heightened anxiety, a constant tormenting worry that the very foundation of life and all that has been created by us may once again be taken away.

Another potent source of anxiety is the pressure to meet societal expectations. In a world that constantly demands more—more success, more productivity, more perfection—the weight of these expectations can be overwhelming. Social media exacerbates this pressure, presenting curated versions of others' lives that seem effortlessly perfect. This comparison trap can lead to feelings of inadequacy, fueling anxiety as we strive to measure up to an unattainable ideal. The fear of failure, of not being enough, can become a relentless source of stress.

Traumatic experiences also leave a lasting imprint on our psyche, often resurfacing as anxiety. The body and mind remember trauma, even when we consciously try to move past it. Flashbacks, nightmares, and hypervigilance are common symptoms, as the brain remains on high alert, ready to respond to perceived threats. This state of hyperarousal can make it difficult to relax, to feel safe, and to trust in the stability of our world.

Environmental factors play a significant role as well. Living in a chaotic or unstable environment can create a perpetual state of anxiety. Noise, overcrowding, and lack of personal space can all contribute to a feeling of being constantly on edge. Additionally, financial instability or job insecurity can create a persistent background hum of worry, as the basic necessities of life feel threatened.

Personal relationships are another arena where anxiety often takes root. Conflict, misunderstandings, and the fear of abandonment can all trigger anxious feelings. The desire for connection and the fear of rejection create a tension that can be difficult to navigate. Trust issues, whether stemming from past betrayals or inherent insecurities, can amplify this anxiety, making it challenging to form and maintain healthy relationships.

Lastly, physical health and lifestyle choices can significantly impact anxiety levels. Poor diet, lack of exercise, and insufficient sleep can all contribute to a heightened state of anxiety. The mind and body are deeply interconnected, and neglecting one often leads to the suffering of the other. Substance abuse, whether it's alcohol, drugs, or even excessive caffeine, can also exacerbate anxiety, creating a vicious cycle of dependency and stress.

Understanding these triggers is a crucial step in managing and mitigating anxiety. By identifying the sources of our stress, we can begin to address them, develop coping strategies, and work towards a more balanced and peaceful state of being.

Anxiety in Daily Life

In the quiet moments of our daily existence, anxiety often sneaks in, uninvited and unannounced. It can manifest in the most mundane tasks, turning routine activities into sources of dread and discomfort. The simple act of getting out of bed in the morning can feel like a monumental task, weighed down by an invisible burden that presses heavily on the chest. This pervasive sense of unease can transform the familiar into the foreboding, making the world seem like an unpredictable and treacherous place.

Walking through the grocery store, one might suddenly feel overwhelmed by the sheer number of choices, the bustling crowd, and the incessant noise. What was once a straightforward errand becomes a labyrinth of potential pitfalls, each decision fraught with the possibility of making a mistake. The mind races, heart pounds, and a cold sweat breaks out, all while trying to maintain a semblance of normalcy. The struggle to appear composed in the face of internal chaos is a daily battle for those grappling with anxiety.

Conversations with colleagues or friends can become minefields, each word carefully chosen to avoid potential embarrassment or misunderstanding. The fear of saying the wrong thing, of being judged or criticized, can be paralyzing. This constant self-monitoring leads to a sense of isolation, as genuine connection becomes increasingly difficult to achieve. The desire to retreat, to escape from the pressure of social interaction, grows stronger with each passing day.

Workplace environments, with their deadlines and expectations, can exacerbate feelings of inadequacy and self-doubt. The pressure to perform, to meet or exceed standards, can create a relentless cycle of stress and worry. Even the most competent and capable individuals can find themselves questioning their abilities, plagued by a persistent fear of failure. This internal struggle often goes unnoticed by others, as the external facade of professionalism masks the turmoil within.

Sleep, once a refuge from the demands of the day, can become elusive. The mind, unable to quiet itself, replays conversations, revisits worries, and anticipates future challenges. The hours tick by, and rest remains just out of reach, leaving one feeling even more vulnerable and exhausted. The lack of restorative sleep only serves to heighten anxiety, creating a vicious cycle that is difficult to break.

Daily life, with its myriad responsibilities and expectations, can feel like a series of obstacles to be navigated. Each task, no matter how small, carries the weight of potential failure or disappointment. The constant vigilance required to manage anxiety can be draining, leaving little energy for joy or spontaneity. The world becomes a place to be endured rather than enjoyed, each day a test of endurance rather than an opportunity for growth.

Yet, within this struggle, there is also a quiet resilience. The act of getting out of bed, of facing the day despite the fear and uncertainty, is a testament to an inner strength that often goes unrecognized. The small victories, the moments of connection, and the instances of calm amidst the storm are all reminders that anxiety, while pervasive, does not define one's entire existence. The journey through daily life with anxiety is a complex and challenging one, but it is also marked by courage and perseverance.

Managing Anxiety

Anxiety often surges through the veins like a relentless tide, especially when one is grappling with grief and depression. It can feel like a shadow, constantly lurking, waiting to pounce at moments of vulnerability. Reflecting on those times when anxiety felt overpowering, it becomes evident how crucial it is to develop strategies to manage it effectively.

One of the most striking realizations is the importance of recognizing the early signs of anxiety. For some, it might be a tightening chest, for others, a racing mind that refuses to quiet down. When these symptoms arise, it's a signal to pause and take stock of the situation. Awareness is the first step in mitigating the overwhelming sensation that anxiety can bring.

Breathing exercises have proven to be a lifeline. Simple, yet profoundly effective, focusing on the breath can anchor the mind and body. Inhale deeply, hold for a moment, and then exhale slowly. This rhythmic pattern can create a sense of calm, allowing a momentary reprieve from the swirling thoughts. It's fascinating how something as innate as breathing can serve as a powerful tool against anxiety.

Another approach that has been invaluable is grounding techniques. When anxiety threatens to spiral out of control, grounding oneself in the present can be immensely helpful. This can be achieved through engaging the senses—touching a textured surface, listening to soothing sounds, or even tasting something tangy. It's a method of bringing oneself back to the here and now, breaking the cycle of anxious thoughts.

The role of physical activity cannot be understated. Exercise, whether it's a brisk walk, a session of yoga, or even dancing around the living room, can release endorphins that naturally combat anxiety. Movement has a way of shaking off the mental cobwebs, providing clarity and a renewed sense of control.

Journaling has also emerged as a therapeutic practice. Writing down thoughts and feelings can serve as a form of release, an unburdening of the mind. It provides a space to explore the roots of anxiety, to understand its triggers, and to reflect on ways to cope. Over time, these written reflections can reveal patterns and insights that might not have been apparent initially.

It's also worth noting the significance of seeking support. Whether it's talking to a trusted friend, joining a support group, or consulting a professional, sharing the burden can make it feel lighter. There is strength in vulnerability, and reaching out can provide not only practical advice but also emotional comfort.

Mindfulness and meditation have gained traction as effective methods to manage anxiety. These practices encourage a focus on the present moment, fostering a sense of peace and acceptance. Guided meditations, in particular, can be a helpful starting point for those new to the practice, offering a structured way to calm the mind.

Diet and sleep are foundational elements that impact anxiety levels. Eating a balanced diet and ensuring adequate rest can significantly influence one's mental state. It's surprising how interconnected physical health is with mental well-being, and maintaining these basics can provide a stronger foundation to face anxiety.

Navigating anxiety in the context of grief and depression is undoubtedly challenging. However, by adopting these strategies and remaining mindful of one's mental state, it's possible to manage anxiety more effectively. Each small step taken towards understanding and addressing anxiety contributes to a larger journey of healing and resilience.

Chapter 3: The Depths of Depression

Recognizing Depression

In those shadowed moments when the weight of the world seems unbearable, there's a subtle shift that can often go unnoticed. Life, once vibrant and full of color, begins to lose its hue. The laughter that once echoed through the halls of your mind now feels distant, a ghostly remnant of happier times. It's not just sadness; it's an overwhelming sense of emptiness, a void that cannot be expressed through any tangible means.

The first step in understanding this complex experience is to acknowledge the signs. Often, these signs are not as overt as one might expect. They creep into daily life, subtly altering perceptions and behaviors. You might find yourself withdrawing from activities that once brought joy. The books that once captivated your imagination now gather dust on the shelf. Social gatherings, which previously were a source of comfort and connection, now feel like insurmountable tasks. These changes, while gradual, are significant.

Sleep patterns begin to change. The sanctuary of night, which once provided rest, now becomes a battleground of restless thoughts and interrupted slumber. Mornings bring a sense of dread, a heaviness that makes the simple act of rising feel like a monumental effort. Appetite, too, is affected. For some, food loses its appeal, each meal becoming a chore rather than a pleasure. For others, it becomes a source of temporary solace, a fleeting escape from the looming darkness.

Emotional responses become unpredictable. Tears may come unbidden, triggered by the smallest of things, or emotions may become muted, a numbness spreading where once there was vibrancy. It's as if a fog has descended, blurring the edges of everything, making it hard to see the world clearly. This fog can be isolating, creating a sense of being cut off from others, even those closest to you.

Physical symptoms often accompany these emotional changes. Persistent fatigue, unexplained aches and pains, and a general sense of malaise can be telltale signs. These physical manifestations are not merely in the mind; they are real and impactful, further complicating the experience of depression.

Recognizing these signs in oneself can be challenging. There's a tendency to dismiss them, to attribute them to stress or a temporary phase. Yet, it's crucial to listen to these signals, to understand that they are not a reflection of personal failure or weakness. They are indicators that something deeper is at play, something that requires attention and care.

For those observing a loved one, the signs may be subtle yet telling. A noticeable withdrawal, a change in demeanor, a loss of enthusiasm for life's pleasures - these are cues that something is amiss. It's important to approach these observations with empathy and understanding, offering support without judgment.

Understanding and recognizing depression is not about labeling or diagnosing; it's about awareness. It's about acknowledging the reality of the experience and the profound impact it has on every aspect of life. This awareness is the first step toward seeking help, toward finding a path through the darkness. It's about opening a dialogue, both with oneself and with others, to bring light to what often feels like an insurmountable void.

Causes of Depression

Understanding the roots of depression often feels like navigating a labyrinthine maze of emotions, thoughts, and experiences. The complexity of this mental health condition lies in the interplay of various factors, both internal and external, that can trigger its onset. It's a tapestry woven with threads of biology, psychology, and environment, each contributing in its unique way.

One cannot overlook the biological underpinnings of depression. Our brains are intricate machines, operating through a delicate balance of chemicals and neurotransmitters. When this balance is disrupted, it can lead to the symptoms we associate with depression. Genetic predisposition plays a significant role here. If a close family member has experienced depression, the likelihood increases.

Psychological factors are equally influential. Our minds are shaped by our experiences, particularly those from our formative years. Traumatic events, such as the loss of a loved one, abuse, or prolonged stress, can leave deep scars. These experiences can alter the way we perceive ourselves and the world around us. Negative thought patterns often develop, creating a cycle of self-doubt and hopelessness. This internal dialogue can be relentless, reinforcing feelings of worthlessness and despair.

The environment in which we live also plays a crucial role. Social factors, such as relationships and community, significantly impact our mental health. Isolation and loneliness are potent contributors to depression. Human beings are inherently social creatures, and a lack of meaningful connections can lead to a profound sense of emptiness. Additionally, societal pressures and cultural expectations can create an overwhelming sense of inadequacy. The constant comparison to others, driven by social media and other platforms, exacerbates these feelings.

Economic instability is another environmental factor that cannot be ignored. Financial stress can lead to persistent worry and anxiety, which, over time, can pave the way to depression. The struggle to meet basic needs, coupled with the fear of an uncertain future, creates a heavy burden that many find difficult to bear. This weight can become suffocating, making it challenging to find joy or purpose in daily life.

Lifestyle choices and habits also contribute to the onset of depression. Poor diet, lack of exercise, and inadequate sleep can negatively affect our mental health. These elements are often interlinked, creating a vicious cycle. For example, depression can lead to insomnia, which in turn exacerbates depressive symptoms. Similarly, a lack of physical activity can reduce the production of endorphins, the body's natural mood lifters.

Substance abuse is another critical factor. While some may turn to alcohol or drugs in an attempt to cope with their feelings, these substances can ultimately worsen depression. They alter brain chemistry and can lead to dependency, creating additional layers of emotional and physical challenges.

Understanding the causes of depression requires a holistic approach. It is not a condition with a single origin but rather a confluence of various elements. Each person's experience is unique, shaped by their biology, personal history, and current circumstances. Recognizing this complexity is crucial in addressing and managing depression effectively. Through empathy and awareness, we can better support those who struggle, helping them navigate their way through the darkness toward a place of healing and hope.

Impact on Life

Grief, anxiety, and depression are not merely abstract concepts to be clinically diagnosed and treated; they are profound experiences that fundamentally alter the fabric of one's existence. As I reflect on the myriad ways these emotions have touched lives, it becomes clear that their impact is both deeply personal and universally recognizable.

Imagine waking up each day with a weight on your chest, an invisible force that makes even the simplest tasks feel insurmountable. This is the reality for many who struggle with these emotional burdens. The once vibrant colors of life seem to fade into a monochromatic palette of despair. Activities that once brought joy now seem hollow, and the laughter that used to echo through the halls of one's mind is replaced by an eerie silence.

Relationships, too, bear the brunt of these emotions. Friends and family may struggle to understand the seemingly inexplicable changes in behavior. The person they once knew seems distant, lost in a fog of sorrow and anxiety. Misunderstandings and frustrations can arise, creating a chasm where there once was closeness. Yet, it is within these relationships that a glimmer of hope often lies. The patience, love, and support of those who care can act as a lifeline, offering moments of respite amidst the chaos.

Professional life is not immune to the effects of grief, anxiety, and depression. Concentration wanes, productivity dips, and the sense of accomplishment that once fueled ambition becomes elusive. The pressure to maintain a façade of normalcy can be overwhelming, leading to a cycle of stress and exhaustion. For some, this may culminate in the difficult decision to step back from their careers, prioritizing mental health over professional advancement.

Physical health, too, is intricately linked with emotional well-being. The body often manifests what the mind cannot express. Sleep patterns become erratic, appetite fluctuates, and chronic fatigue sets in. The immune system may weaken, making one more susceptible to illnesses. This interplay between mind and body underscores the importance of holistic approaches to healing, recognizing that one cannot be treated in isolation from the other.

Yet, amidst the darkness, there are moments of profound clarity and growth. Grief, anxiety, and depression force a reevaluation of priorities, prompting a deeper understanding of oneself and one's place in the world. They challenge individuals to confront their vulnerabilities, fostering resilience and empathy. The journey through these emotions is not linear, and there are no quick fixes. However, each small victory, whether it be getting out of bed on a particularly difficult day or finding solace in a moment of mindfulness, is a testament to the strength of the human spirit.

In this reflective space, it becomes evident that the impact of grief, anxiety, and depression is multifaceted. They shape lives in ways that are both visible and hidden, influencing thoughts, behaviors, and relationships. While the journey may be arduous, it is also a testament to the resilience and enduring hope that lies within each individual. Through understanding and compassion, both for oneself and others, the path forward becomes a little clearer, illuminated by the shared experiences of those who have walked it before.

Path to Recovery

The days following a significant loss or a period of profound anxiety and depression often feel like navigating through an uncharted territory. Each moment is imbued with a sense of unfamiliarity, and the simplest of tasks can seem insurmountable. One might find themselves questioning if they will ever return to a semblance of normalcy or if the weight of their emotions will perpetually anchor them to this state of limbo.

Reflecting on this period, it becomes evident that the first step toward healing is acknowledgment. It's not merely about recognizing the presence of grief, anxiety, or depression, but about understanding its depth and complexity. These emotions are not fleeting; they are deeply rooted and multifaceted. By acknowledging their presence, one grants themselves the permission to feel and, importantly, to heal.

During this time, it's crucial to cultivate a space where feelings can be expressed without judgment. This space might be found in the solitude of a quiet room, the pages of a journal, or the comforting presence of a trusted friend or therapist. The act of verbalizing or writing down thoughts and emotions can be profoundly therapeutic. It allows for a release, a way to externalize the internal chaos and begin to make sense of it.

One might also find solace in small routines and rituals. These seemingly mundane activities can serve as anchors, providing a sense of stability amidst emotional upheaval. Whether it's a daily walk, a cup of tea in the morning, or a few minutes of meditation, these practices can offer a momentary respite and a semblance of control.

It's important to remember that healing is not linear. There will be days of progress, where the weight feels a little lighter, and days where it feels like the sorrow is all-encompassing. Both types of days are part of the process. On the more challenging days, it can be helpful to remind oneself of the progress made, no matter how small. Each step forward is significant, even if it's followed by a step back.

Connecting with others who have experienced similar emotions can also be incredibly beneficial. Support groups, whether in-person or online, provide a sense of community and understanding. Knowing that others have walked a similar path and have found ways to cope can be both comforting and inspiring. It serves as a reminder that while the journey is deeply personal, it is not one that must be walked alone.

Professional help should never be underestimated. Therapy, whether cognitive-behavioral, psychodynamic, or another form, offers tools and strategies to manage and understand emotions. Medication may also be a necessary component for some, providing the biochemical support needed to navigate through particularly tough periods. There is no shame in seeking help; it is a sign of strength and a crucial step toward recovery.

Throughout this period, self-compassion is vital. The tendency to judge oneself harshly or to feel guilty for not "moving on" quickly enough can be detrimental. It's essential to treat oneself with the same kindness and understanding that one would offer a dear friend going through a similar experience.

Healing from grief, anxiety, and depression is a deeply personal and often painful process. However, by acknowledging emotions, seeking support, and practicing self-compassion, one can begin to find moments of peace and clarity. These moments, however fleeting, are the building blocks of recovery. They are evidence that, despite the darkness, there is a way forward.

Chapter 4: Universal Guidance

Connecting with the Universe

The vastness of the universe often feels like a daunting reminder of how small and insignificant our personal struggles can seem. Yet, in moments of profound grief, anxiety, and depression, there is a peculiar solace to be found in this boundless expanse. It is a paradoxical comfort, knowing that amidst the chaos and pain, there exists a larger, unfathomable cosmos that continues to function, to breathe, and to evolve.

In the depths of sorrow, when the weight of loss feels unbearable, lifting our gaze to the stars can provide a strange kind of relief. The night sky, with its myriad of twinkling lights, serves as a gentle reminder that life persists, even in the darkest of times. Each star, a distant sun, has witnessed the birth and death of countless worlds, experienced eons of change, and yet remains a constant beacon in the sky. This enduring presence can offer a sense of stability, a reminder that while our pain is real and immediate, it is also part of a much larger tapestry.

Anxiety often roots itself in the fear of the unknown, the uncontrollable. The universe, with its infinite mysteries, embodies the ultimate unknown. However, rather than exacerbating our fears, contemplating the cosmos can provide a unique perspective. The realization that we are mere specks in a vast, ever-expanding universe can be humbling. This humbleness has the power to shift our focus away from our immediate concerns, allowing us to see them in a different light. The cosmos, indifferent to our worries, continues its grand dance of creation and destruction, a dance we are privileged to witness, even if only for a fleeting moment.

Depression, with its heavy cloak of despair, often makes the world feel small and confined. The universe, in contrast, is a reminder of infinite possibilities. The sheer scale of it, the beauty of galaxies swirling millions of light-years away, can ignite a spark of awe. This awe, even if momentary, can pierce through the fog of depression, offering a glimpse of something beyond our immediate suffering. It serves as a reminder that there is more to existence than our current pain, that there are wonders and mysteries yet to be explored.

Connecting with the universe does not require a deep understanding of astrophysics or cosmology. It is an invitation to step outside, to look up, and to allow oneself to be enveloped by the vastness of the night sky. It is about finding moments of stillness, where the mind can wander among the stars, free from the constraints of earthly troubles. This connection, though seemingly simple, can be profoundly healing. It offers a sense of belonging to something greater, a reminder that we are part of an intricate, interconnected web of existence.

In moments of grief, anxiety, and depression, the universe serves as a silent companion. Its vastness is a canvas upon which we can project our hopes, fears, and dreams. By connecting with this infinite expanse, we can find a sense of peace, a moment of respite, and perhaps, a glimmer of hope. This connection, fragile yet powerful, is a testament to the resilience of the human spirit and its unending quest for meaning amidst the stars.

Past Life Connections

The intricate web of our emotional landscape is often more complex than it appears at first glance. When dealing with grief, anxiety, and depression, one might find that the roots of these emotions extend beyond the present moment, reaching into the depths of our past experiences. This concept, though subtle, can be a profound revelation in understanding and healing our current emotional struggles.

Reflecting on the past, one can uncover significant events or relationships that have left an indelible mark on our psyche. These past life connections are not necessarily tied to the metaphysical idea of reincarnation but rather to the impactful moments and people who have shaped our emotional world. These connections can manifest in various ways, such as unresolved grief from a lost relationship, lingering anxiety from a traumatic event, or persistent depression rooted in long-standing feelings of inadequacy or rejection.

In the quiet moments of introspection, we might recall a specific person or experience that continues to influence our emotional state. Perhaps it was a childhood friend whose sudden departure left a void, or a family member whose expectations created an enduring sense of pressure. These memories, often buried under the busyness of everyday life, can resurface during times of emotional distress, demanding our attention and resolution.

Understanding the significance of these past connections requires a willingness to delve into our history with an open and compassionate heart. It involves acknowledging the pain, fear, or sadness that these experiences have wrought and recognizing their ongoing impact on our mental health. This process is not about dwelling on the past but rather about bringing to light the hidden influences that shape our present emotions.

By identifying these connections, we can begin to untangle the complex web of our feelings. For instance, someone experiencing anxiety might trace their fears back to a time when they felt unsafe or unsupported, revealing a pattern that has persisted into adulthood. Similarly, an individual grappling with depression might discover that their sense of worthlessness stems from repeated instances of criticism or neglect in their formative years.

This reflective practice can be both enlightening and therapeutic. It allows us to see our current struggles through a different lens, fostering a deeper understanding of ourselves and our emotional responses. Moreover, it opens the door to healing, as recognizing these past influences provides an opportunity to address and resolve them.

Healing from these past connections often involves a combination of self-reflection, therapy, and, importantly, self-compassion. Therapy can offer a structured environment to explore these issues, guided by a professional who can help navigate the complex emotions that arise. Self-compassion, on the other hand, is about being kind to ourselves as we confront these painful memories, understanding that our past experiences do not define our worth.

In this journey of self-discovery, it is essential to be patient and gentle with oneself. Emotional healing is not a linear process; it involves setbacks and progress, moments of clarity, and times of confusion. However, by acknowledging and understanding our past life connections, we take a crucial step towards unraveling the intricate tapestry of our emotions, paving the way for a more peaceful and fulfilling present.

Embracing the Present Moment

In the midst of grief, anxiety, and depression, it is often the simplest moments that provide a lifeline to sanity. The present moment, with all its rawness and authenticity, is a refuge from the labyrinth of thoughts and emotions that can overwhelm us. It is here, in the now, that we can find a semblance of peace and clarity.

One of the most profound realizations in the throes of emotional turmoil is the importance of grounding oneself in the present. When the mind is racing with worries about the future or regrets about the past, it is easy to be swept away in a tide of negative emotions. However, by anchoring ourselves to the present, we can begin to unravel the knots of our inner turmoil.

Mindfulness, the practice of being fully present and engaged in the current moment, offers a powerful tool for navigating the stormy seas of grief, anxiety, and depression. It invites us to observe our thoughts and feelings without judgment, allowing us to see them for what they are: transient and ever-changing. Through mindfulness, we can learn to detach from the incessant chatter of the mind and find solace in the simplicity of the present.

Breathing, an act so fundamental to our existence, becomes a gateway to the present moment. By focusing on the rhythm of our breath, we can bring our attention back to the here and now. Each inhale and exhale serves as a reminder that we are alive, that we are capable of experiencing this moment, no matter how painful it may be.

Nature, too, offers a sanctuary for those struggling with emotional distress. The rustling of leaves, the chirping of birds, the gentle caress of the wind—these natural phenomena remind us of the beauty and continuity of life. In nature, we can find moments of respite, where the weight of our sorrows is momentarily lifted, and we can simply be.

Engaging in creative activities can also be a powerful way to connect with the present. Whether it's painting, writing, dancing, or playing an instrument, creative expression allows us to channel our emotions in a constructive and healing manner. In these moments of creation, we are fully immersed in the act, free from the burdens of the past and the uncertainties of the future.

It's important to acknowledge that embracing the present moment does not mean denying or suppressing our pain. Rather, it is about allowing ourselves to feel our emotions fully, without being consumed by them. It is about finding a balance between acknowledging our suffering and recognizing the moments of peace and beauty that exist alongside it.

Gratitude, even in the darkest of times, can be a beacon of light. By consciously seeking out and appreciating the small blessings in our lives, we can shift our focus from what we have lost to what we still have. This shift in perspective can provide a much-needed sense of hope and resilience.

In the end, the present moment is all we truly have. It is a reminder that life is a series of fleeting instances, each one an opportunity to experience, to learn, and to grow. By embracing the present moment, we can navigate the complexities of grief, anxiety, and depression with a sense of grace and acceptance.

Understanding Prarabdha

Reflecting on the intricate tapestry of our lives, it becomes clear that there's a mysterious force at play, one that shapes our experiences in ways both subtle and profound. This force, often referred to as Prarabdha in ancient wisdom traditions, signifies the portion of our past karma that is ripe and ready to be experienced in this lifetime. It is the thread that weaves through the fabric of our existence, influencing our circumstances, actions, and the emotional landscapes we navigate.

In the context of grief, anxiety, and depression, understanding Prarabdha offers a unique perspective. It suggests that some of the emotional challenges we face are not merely random occurrences but are intricately linked to our past actions and decisions. This perspective does not intend to minimize the pain or struggle associated with these emotions. Instead, it provides a framework for understanding that can lead to deeper acceptance and compassion for oneself.

Consider grief, for instance. The loss of a loved one can feel overwhelmingly unjust and senseless. Through the lens of Prarabdha, such a loss might be seen as part of a larger, cosmic balance. This doesn't diminish the heartache but offers a way to find meaning in the suffering. It invites us to reflect on the transient nature of life and the interconnectedness of all beings. By recognizing that our current sorrow is part of a broader narrative, we can begin to find solace in the continuity of existence and the enduring connections that transcend physical presence.

Anxiety, too, can be viewed through this lens. The persistent worry and fear that characterize anxiety may stem from unresolved issues and past experiences that have carried over into the present. Understanding Prarabdha encourages us to explore these underlying karmic threads. It suggests that our current state of mind is not a permanent flaw but a temporary manifestation of deeper, historical patterns. This realization can be empowering, as it shifts the focus from self-blame to self-inquiry. By delving into the roots of our anxiety, we can uncover insights that lead to healing and growth.

Depression, with its profound sense of hopelessness and despair, often feels like an insurmountable barrier. Viewing depression through the concept of Prarabdha can offer a glimmer of hope. It implies that our darkest moments are part of a necessary process, one that ultimately contributes to our spiritual evolution. This perspective encourages patience and self-compassion. It reminds us that even in the depths of depression, there is potential for transformation. By accepting our current state without judgment, we can begin to cultivate the inner strength needed to navigate through the darkness.

Understanding Prarabdha is not about resigning to fate or relinquishing control over our lives. Rather, it is an invitation to engage with our experiences more deeply and consciously. It encourages us to view our emotional struggles not as burdens to be borne but as opportunities for growth and understanding. By doing so, we can transform our relationship with grief, anxiety, and depression, finding within them the seeds of resilience and wisdom.

In this light, every moment of suffering becomes a stepping stone on the path to greater self-awareness and inner peace. The concept of Prarabdha reminds us that we are not alone in our struggles; we are part of a vast, interconnected web of existence, where every experience, no matter how painful, has its place and purpose. This understanding can be a source of profound comfort and strength as we navigate the complexities of our emotional lives.

Chapter 5: Karmic Balance

The Concept of Karma

Karma is a concept deeply rooted in various spiritual traditions, often misunderstood and oversimplified in modern discourse. It is not merely about good deeds yielding good results and bad deeds leading to suffering. Rather, it is a complex, nuanced principle that encapsulates the intricate web of cause and effect governing our lives. In reflecting upon karma, one can find profound insights into the nature of grief, anxiety, and depression.

Life, with its myriad experiences, constantly presents us with challenges that test our emotional and mental resilience. When we encounter grief, it is easy to feel overwhelmed by a sense of helplessness. The sting of loss, whether it be the death of a loved one, the end of a relationship, or the loss of a dream, can be debilitating. It is in these moments of profound sorrow that the concept of karma can offer a different perspective. Rather than viewing grief as an arbitrary punishment or a stroke of bad luck, considering it as a part of the karmic cycle can provide a sense of meaning and continuity. It suggests that our experiences are interconnected, a result of past actions and decisions, and that even in our deepest sorrow, there is potential for growth and understanding.

Anxiety, characterized by a constant state of worry and fear, often feels like an uncontrollable force. The mind races with thoughts of what might go wrong, creating a relentless cycle of dread. By reflecting on karma, we can begin to see anxiety not as a random affliction but as an opportunity to examine the causes and conditions that have led to this state. It encourages a mindful investigation of our actions, thoughts, and intentions. What patterns have we established in our lives that contribute to our anxiety? How can we cultivate more positive habits and thought processes to create a more peaceful state of being? This introspective approach can transform anxiety from a paralyzing force into a catalyst for personal growth and self-awareness.

Depression, with its pervasive sense of hopelessness and despair, can make it seem as though life has lost all meaning. The weight of sadness can be so heavy that it feels insurmountable. Here, the concept of karma can serve as a beacon of light. It reminds us that our current state is not permanent, but part of an ever-changing cycle. This perspective can be empowering, as it suggests that through conscious effort and mindful living, we have the ability to influence our future experiences. By acknowledging the karmic roots of our depression, we can take steps to address and heal the underlying causes, whether they be unresolved trauma, negative thought patterns, or harmful behaviors.

In contemplating karma, it is essential to recognize that it is not a deterministic force but a dynamic interplay of actions and consequences. It encourages personal responsibility and the understanding that we have the power to shape our destiny through our choices. This realization can be incredibly liberating, offering a sense of agency and hope even in the face of grief, anxiety, and depression. By integrating the principles of karma into our lives, we can cultivate a deeper awareness of our actions and their impact, fostering a more compassionate and mindful approach to our mental and emotional wellbeing.

Balancing Past Actions

Reflecting on the myriad of memories that string together the tapestry of our lives, there lies a delicate balance between what was and what is. Life, in its unpredictable nature, often leaves us grappling with decisions made in the heat of the moment, lingering regrets, and the weight of actions taken or not taken. In the quiet moments, these reflections can stir a tumultuous sea of emotions, particularly for those navigating the stormy waters of grief, anxiety, and depression.

When looking back on past actions, the human mind has a tendency to amplify mistakes, casting a shadow over the present. This self-imposed burden can lead to a cyclical pattern of negative thinking, where one's worth and identity become entangled with perceived failures. However, it is essential to recognize that these reflections, while painful, also hold the key to understanding and healing.

Acknowledging past actions without judgment is a crucial step. This involves observing these moments as they are, without the harsh lens of self-criticism. It's about seeing the decisions made through the eyes of compassion, understanding that every choice was influenced by the circumstances, knowledge, and emotional state at that time. This compassionate perspective allows for a more balanced view, where the past is seen not as a series of mistakes, but as a collection of experiences that have shaped one's current self.

There is also a profound strength in identifying and accepting responsibility for one's actions. This acceptance is not about assigning blame or wallowing in guilt, but rather about recognizing the impact of those actions on oneself and others. It is through this recognition that one can begin to make amends, whether that be through direct action or through internal reconciliation.

Forgiveness, both of oneself and of others, plays a pivotal role in this process. Holding onto resentment or guilt can perpetuate feelings of grief and anxiety, creating a barrier to moving forward. Forgiveness is not about condoning past actions, but about releasing the hold they have on one's emotional well-being. It's a conscious decision to let go of the anguish tied to those moments, allowing for the possibility of peace and growth.

The practice of mindfulness can be particularly beneficial when dealing with the repercussions of past actions. By staying present and focused on the current moment, it becomes easier to detach from the relentless replay of past events. Mindfulness encourages a state of being where one can observe thoughts and feelings without becoming overwhelmed by them. This detachment provides a clearer perspective and fosters a more balanced emotional state.

Seeking support from others can also be a vital part of this journey. Sharing one's reflections with trusted friends, family, or a therapist can offer new insights and alleviate the sense of isolation that often accompanies these feelings. External perspectives can provide clarity and help in reframing past actions in a more constructive light.

Balancing past actions involves a delicate interplay of acceptance, forgiveness, and mindful reflection. It is through this balance that one can begin to heal, transforming past pain into a source of strength and resilience. The journey may be fraught with challenges, but it also holds the promise of a deeper understanding of oneself and a renewed sense of peace.

Karma in Relationships

Relationships often serve as mirrors reflecting our innermost thoughts, beliefs, and emotional patterns. They are the crucibles where karma is most vividly and intensely experienced. It's within these intimate connections that the interplay of past actions, both our own and those of others, manifests most clearly. The dynamics we encounter within relationships can often be traced back to unresolved issues from our past, which resurface in the present, demanding attention and resolution.

Consider the moments when a seemingly trivial argument with a loved one spirals into a deeply emotional confrontation. It might feel as though you're reacting to the present situation, but often, these intense emotions are tethered to past experiences. These patterns, etched into our psyche, replay themselves, offering repeated opportunities for healing and growth.

Recognizing these patterns is the first step toward breaking free from the cycle of karmic entanglement.

In relationships, karma can manifest as recurring conflicts, emotional triggers, or even the types of partners we attract. For instance, someone who feels perpetually unworthy might attract partners who reinforce this belief, thereby perpetuating a cycle of emotional pain. This isn't a punishment but rather a call to address and heal the underlying wounds. By facing these issues head-on, we can transform our relationships into spaces of profound healing and mutual growth.

Understanding karma in relationships also involves recognizing the role of forgiveness. Holding onto grudges or past hurts only serves to bind us more tightly to the karmic cycle. Forgiveness, on the other hand, allows for the release of negative energy and the creation of space for positive growth. This doesn't mean condoning harmful behavior but rather choosing to let go of the emotional burden it imposes. In doing so, we free ourselves and our partners from the chains of past actions, allowing for a more harmonious and loving connection.

Communication is another crucial aspect of navigating karmic relationships. Honest and open dialogue can illuminate hidden patterns and provide insights into the deeper issues at play. By expressing our feelings and listening to our partners without judgment, we create a safe space for mutual understanding and healing. This process requires vulnerability and courage, but the rewards are profound, fostering deeper intimacy and connection.

It's also essential to approach relationships with a sense of compassion and empathy. Recognizing that our partners are also dealing with their own karmic baggage can foster a sense of solidarity and mutual support. By supporting each other through these challenges, we can transform our relationships into powerful catalysts for personal and spiritual growth.

Self-reflection plays a pivotal role in this journey. Taking the time to introspect and understand our own contributions to the karmic dynamics in our relationships is crucial. This involves acknowledging our own flaws and taking responsibility for our actions. By doing so, we empower ourselves to make conscious choices that break the cycle of negative karma and pave the way for healthier, more fulfilling relationships.

Relationships, in their essence, are opportunities for profound learning and growth. They challenge us, push our boundaries, and ultimately, help us evolve. By understanding and addressing the karmic elements within our relationships, we can transform them into sanctuaries of healing and mutual evolution. Embracing this perspective allows us to navigate the complexities of relationships with grace and wisdom, fostering deeper connections and a more profound sense of inner peace.

Healing Through Karma

Reflecting on the intricate interplay between our actions and their repercussions, one cannot help but ponder the concept of karma. This ancient principle, rooted in various spiritual traditions, suggests that our thoughts, actions, and intentions create a ripple effect that shapes our experiences. When grappling with grief, anxiety, and depression, it is worth considering how this cosmic law might offer a pathway to healing.

Karma, often misunderstood as mere cause and effect, delves deeper into the moral and spiritual dimensions of our lives. It posits that our present circumstances are a reflection of past deeds, not as a form of punishment, but as an opportunity for growth and learning. This perspective can be both liberating and daunting. It invites us to take responsibility for our emotional states while offering a framework to understand and transcend them.

In the throes of grief, the weight of loss can feel unbearable. The heartache and sorrow can seem like an insurmountable burden. Yet, through the lens of karma, this pain may be perceived as part of a larger tapestry, woven with threads of past actions and choices. This does not diminish the validity of our suffering but rather contextualizes it within a broader spiritual narrative. By acknowledging the karmic roots of our grief, we might find a way to honor our pain while seeking the lessons it imparts.

Anxiety, with its relentless grip on our minds, often leaves us feeling powerless and overwhelmed. The constant worry and fear can erode our sense of self and well-being. Karma encourages us to examine the origins of our anxiety, be it from past experiences or unresolved issues. This introspective journey can reveal patterns that perpetuate our distress, offering a chance to break free from the cycle. By aligning our actions with positive intentions and compassionate deeds, we can gradually transform the karmic energy that fuels our anxiety, fostering a sense of peace and resilience.

Depression, a profound and pervasive darkness, can obscure our ability to see hope or purpose. It is a state where the weight of existence feels crushing, and the light at the end of the tunnel seems distant. Through the karmic perspective, depression may be viewed as a call to delve deeper into our inner selves, to confront and heal the wounds that lie beneath the surface. This process is neither quick nor easy, but it is a journey of profound self-discovery and transformation. By cultivating mindfulness and engaging in acts of kindness, we can generate positive karma that gradually lifts the veil of despair.

Karma teaches us that our present is not a fixed destiny but a multifold reaction of past actions and current choices. It empowers us to take conscious steps towards healing, recognizing that each thought, word, and deed contributes to our overall well-being. In the face of grief, anxiety, and depression, this awareness can be a beacon of hope, guiding us towards a future shaped by compassion, understanding, and inner peace.

Engaging with karma as a healing tool requires patience and perseverance. It is an ongoing process of reflection and action, where every moment presents an opportunity to create positive change. By embracing this philosophy, we can transform our suffering into a catalyst for growth, finding solace and strength in the knowledge that we are active participants in our own healing journey.

Chapter 6: Spiritual Healing

Accepting Painful Realities

When faced with grief, anxiety, or depression, the initial step often involves confronting the truth of the situation. It is a moment that feels like a sharp intake of breath, a jolt of cold reality that makes one acutely aware of the weight they carry. Denial can be a soothing balm, a temporary escape, but the path to healing begins with acknowledging the pain.

The mind has a remarkable ability to create illusions, to wrap itself in layers of denial and distraction. However, these layers, while protective, can also hinder progress. Confronting painful realities requires peeling back these layers, a process that is neither swift nor easy. It demands courage and a willingness to face discomfort.

In these moments, it is crucial to allow oneself to feel. Emotions like sadness, anger, and confusion are not enemies to be vanquished but signals that something significant has transpired. They are part of the human experience, markers on the map of one's emotional landscape. Ignoring them only serves to prolong the suffering.

Reflection becomes a powerful tool in this process. Taking the time to sit with one's thoughts and feelings can provide clarity. Journaling, for instance, can be a way to give voice to the turmoil within. Words on a page can transform abstract emotions into something tangible, something that can be examined and understood.

It is also important to recognize that accepting painful realities does not mean resigning oneself to them. Acceptance is not synonymous with giving up. Instead, it is about acknowledging the truth of the situation and understanding that it is a part of one's journey. It is about finding a way to live with the pain, to integrate it into one's life in a way that allows for growth and healing.

Support from others can be invaluable during this time. Sharing one's burden can lighten the load, even if only slightly. Friends, family, or support groups can provide a sense of connection and understanding. They can offer different perspectives and remind one that they are not alone in their struggles.

Professional help, such as therapy, can also be an essential part of this process. A therapist can provide a safe space to explore difficult emotions and offer tools and strategies for coping. They can help one navigate the complex landscape of grief, anxiety, and depression, providing guidance and support along the way.

It is also worth noting that this process is not linear. There will be days when the pain feels overwhelming, and others when it seems more manageable. There will be moments of progress and moments of setback. This ebb and flow is natural and does not signify failure. It is simply part of the journey.

Through this process, one may discover a resilience they did not know they possessed. The act of facing and accepting painful realities can be empowering. It can lead to a deeper understanding of oneself and a greater appreciation for the strength found in vulnerability.

In the end, accepting painful realities is about making peace with the past and finding a way to move forward. It is about acknowledging the depth of one's pain and recognizing the potential for healing and growth that lies within.

Manifestation of Inner World

In the stillness of our minds, grief, anxiety, and depression often take root, weaving intricate patterns that reflect our innermost fears and sorrows. These emotions, though deeply personal, manifest in ways that are both profound and universal. They shape our perceptions, color our experiences, and influence our interactions with the world around us.

Grief, in its essence, is a response to loss. It is a raw, visceral emotion that can leave us feeling untethered and adrift. The loss of a loved one, a cherished dream, or even a way of life can trigger a cascade of emotions that are difficult to navigate. This emotional turbulence can manifest in a myriad of ways: a lingering sense of sadness, a heaviness in the chest, or an overwhelming feeling of emptiness. These physical and emotional symptoms are not just reactions to the loss itself but are also reflections of the deep connection we had with what is now gone.

Anxiety, on the other hand, is often a response to uncertainty and perceived threats. It is an emotion that can creep in slowly, like a fog, or strike suddenly, like a bolt of lightning. When anxiety takes hold, it can distort our perception of reality, making us hyper-aware of potential dangers and catastrophes. This heightened state of vigilance can lead to physical symptoms such as a racing heart, shortness of breath, and muscle tension. These manifestations are the body's way of preparing for a threat, real or imagined. Yet, in the absence of a tangible danger, this constant state of alertness can become debilitating.

Depression, perhaps the most pervasive of the three is a profound sense of despair and hopelessness. It is not merely a transient feeling of sadness but a deep-seated emotion that can pervade every aspect of our lives. Depression can alter our thoughts, making us believe that we are worthless, unlovable, and incapable of change. This negative self-perception can lead to a withdrawal from activities and relationships that once brought joy and fulfillment. The physical manifestations of depression can include fatigue, changes in appetite, and disrupted sleep patterns. These symptoms are not just byproducts of the emotional pain but are also indicative of the body's struggle to cope with the overwhelming burden of despair.

The manifestation of these inner worlds is not always visible to others. Often, those who suffer from grief, anxiety, and depression do so in silence, masking their pain behind a facade of normalcy. The external world may continue to move forward, oblivious to the turmoil within. This disconnect between the inner and outer worlds can exacerbate feelings of isolation and loneliness, making it even more challenging to seek help and support.

Understanding the manifestation of these emotions is crucial in addressing their impact on our lives. It requires a compassionate and empathetic approach, one that acknowledges the depth of the pain while also recognizing the strength and resilience of the human spirit. By exploring and validating these inner experiences, we can begin to find ways to navigate the complexities of grief, anxiety, and depression, and ultimately, to heal.

Self-Affirmation Techniques

In the throes of grief, anxiety, and depression, the mind can become a relentless critic, echoing doubts and fears that magnify our pain. It is in these moments of vulnerability that self-affirmation techniques can serve as a beacon, guiding us toward a more compassionate view of ourselves. Self-affirmation, at its core, involves recognizing and reinforcing the positive aspects of our identity, values, and experiences. It is not a superficial exercise but a profound practice that nurtures inner strength and resilience.

One powerful self-affirmation technique is the daily practice of writing positive statements about oneself. This can be as simple as jotting down three things you appreciate about yourself each morning. These affirmations might focus on your strengths, past achievements, or qualities you value. By consistently engaging in this practice, you begin to rewire your brain, shifting the focus from self-criticism to self-compassion. This shift can gradually alleviate the weight of negative emotions, creating a foundation for healing.

Another effective method is the use of mirror affirmations. Standing before a mirror, look into your own eyes and speak kindly to yourself. This might feel uncomfortable or even silly at first, but it can be incredibly powerful. Affirmations such as "I am worthy of love and respect," "I am strong and capable," or "I deserve happiness" can slowly transform the way you perceive yourself. The physical act of speaking these words aloud reinforces their impact, helping to internalize these positive beliefs.

Engaging in self-affirmation also involves recognizing and celebrating small victories. In the midst of grief or depression, it is easy to overlook progress or dismiss achievements. Yet, acknowledging even the smallest steps forward can bolster your sense of self-worth. Whether it is getting out of bed on a particularly tough day, completing a task, or reaching out for support, these actions deserve recognition. Keeping a journal of these accomplishments can serve as a tangible reminder of your resilience and growth.

Connecting with core values is another integral aspect of self-affirmation. Reflect on what truly matters to you—whether it is kindness, creativity, honesty, or any other value. Identify ways in which you have embodied these values in your life. This reflection can be particularly grounding, providing a sense of purpose and direction even in the midst of emotional turmoil. By aligning your actions with your values, you reinforce a positive self-identity that can withstand the challenges of grief and depression.

Incorporating self-affirmation into your daily routine can also involve mindfulness practices. Mindfulness encourages a non-judgmental awareness of the present moment, allowing you to observe your thoughts and feelings without being overwhelmed by them. This practice can be complemented by self-affirming statements that acknowledge your current struggles while affirming your inherent worth. For example, during a mindfulness meditation, you might silently repeat affirmations such as "I am doing my best," or "I am deserving of peace."

Self-affirmation is not a panacea, but it is a vital tool in the broader journey of healing. It requires patience and consistency, and its effects may be gradual. However, by consciously nurturing a positive self-view, you cultivate a source of inner strength that can support you through the darkest times. In the face of grief, anxiety, and depression, self-affirmation techniques offer a pathway to reclaiming your sense of worth and resilience.

Journey Towards Wholeness

The path through grief, anxiety, and depression is often fraught with overwhelming emotions and profound challenges. It is a deeply personal experience, marked by moments of despair and glimmers of hope. As one navigates this tumultuous landscape, the importance of seeking wholeness becomes evident.

Wholeness, in this context, is not about an absence of pain but rather an integration of experiences that fosters healing and growth.

Reflecting on one's journey through these emotional landscapes, it becomes clear that self-compassion is a crucial element. In the throes of grief, anxiety, or depression, it is easy to fall into patterns of self-criticism and blame. However, recognizing that these emotions are a natural response to life's difficulties can pave the way for a more gentle and understanding approach towards oneself. Embracing self-compassion means acknowledging one's pain and offering the same kindness that one would extend to a dear friend.

Another vital aspect is the role of connection. Isolation often exacerbates feelings of despair, making it crucial to reach out and connect with others. Whether through professional therapy, support groups, or trusted friends and family, sharing one's experiences can provide a sense of relief and validation. It is in these connections that one finds the strength to continue moving forward, even when the path seems insurmountable.

Mindfulness and present-moment awareness also serve as powerful tools in this process. By focusing on the present, rather than ruminating on the past or worrying about the future, one can find moments of peace amidst the chaos. Practices such as meditation, deep breathing, and mindful movement can anchor one in the present, providing a respite from the relentless onslaught of negative thoughts and emotions.

Additionally, finding meaning in the midst of suffering can be transformative. This does not imply that one must find a silver lining in every painful experience but rather that one can seek understanding and growth from these challenges. Engaging in creative pursuits, volunteering, or even journaling can help process emotions and uncover deeper insights about oneself and the world.

It is also essential to recognize that healing is not linear. There will be setbacks and days when the weight of emotions feels unbearable. On such days, it is vital to remember that progress is not measured by the absence of pain but by the resilience to face it. Allowing oneself to feel the full spectrum of emotions without judgment is a testament to one's strength and humanity.

Lastly, cultivating hope plays a significant role. Hope is not about blind optimism but about believing in the possibility of better days. It is the quiet assurance that, despite the current struggles, there is potential for joy, connection, and fulfillment. Nurturing this hope can be as simple as setting small, achievable goals or as profound as envisioning a life where pain coexists with moments of genuine happiness.

In traversing through the course of grief, anxiety, and depression, one discovers that wholeness is not a destination but an ongoing process. It is about weaving together the threads of pain and joy, loss and growth, despair and hope, to create a tapestry that reflects the full richness of the human experience. Through self-compassion, connection, mindfulness, meaning, resilience, and hope, one can find a sense of wholeness that sustains and nurtures the spirit.

Chapter 7: Self-Healing Practices

Daily Self-Work

Every morning, as the first light of dawn gently filters through the curtains, we have a choice. Each day presents an opportunity to engage in the delicate practice of self-work, a commitment to nurturing our mental and emotional well-being amidst the throes of grief, anxiety, and depression. The simple act of rising from bed can feel insurmountable, yet it is a powerful testament to our resilience and willingness to heal.

The initial moments of the day can set the tone for the hours that follow. It is in these early stages that we can introduce practices designed to center and ground ourselves. A few minutes of mindful breathing, allowing the rhythm of inhalation and exhalation to anchor us, can create a sense of calm. This practice doesn't demand perfection; it invites presence. Often, our minds are cluttered with thoughts of past regrets or future worries.

By focusing on the breath, we cultivate a moment of peace within the storm.

Journaling can serve as another powerful tool. Writing down our thoughts, feelings, and experiences allows us to externalize what is often an internal chaos. It is not about crafting perfect sentences but about creating a safe space for self-expression. Through the act of writing, we can begin to understand the patterns in our emotions and identify triggers that exacerbate our pain. This self-awareness is the first step in reclaiming a sense of control.

Physical movement, however gentle, can also play a crucial role. Whether it's a short walk in the park, stretching exercises, or a more structured workout, moving our bodies helps release endorphins, the body's natural mood elevators. Engaging in physical activity can break the cycle of inertia that often accompanies depression and anxiety. It serves as a reminder that we are alive, capable of movement and change.

Connecting with others, even in small ways, can be profoundly healing. A brief conversation with a friend or family member, sharing a cup of tea, or simply being in the presence of another person can alleviate the sense of isolation that often accompanies grief and depression. Human connection can be a mirror, reflecting back to us our worth and the simple truth that we are not alone in our struggles.

Setting small, achievable goals can provide a sense of accomplishment and forward momentum. These goals need not be grand; they can be as simple as making the bed, preparing a healthy meal, or reading a few pages of a book. Each completed task is a victory, a step towards reclaiming our lives from the grip of despair.

It's important to acknowledge and honor our emotions without judgment. There will be days when it feels impossible to engage in any of these practices, and that's okay. Self-compassion is paramount. Recognizing that healing is not linear and that setbacks are a natural part of the process can alleviate the pressure to always be "doing better."

Engaging in daily self-work is an act of courage and love. It is a commitment to ourselves, a declaration that our well-being matters. Through small, consistent efforts, we can begin to navigate the complex landscape of grief, anxiety, and depression, finding moments of peace and clarity amidst the turmoil. These practices, though simple, can become the building blocks of a more resilient and hopeful self.

Techniques for Resisting Situations

Finding oneself in the throes of grief, anxiety, or depression can feel like being caught in an endless storm, where the horizon is obscured and every step is a struggle against the wind. In such moments, it is essential to have tools at one's disposal, techniques that can be employed to resist the overwhelming weight of these emotions. These techniques are not about denying or avoiding feelings but about creating a space where one can breathe, reflect, and begin to heal.

One of the most effective techniques is mindfulness, a practice that encourages staying present in the moment. Mindfulness can be as simple as focusing on one's breath, feeling the air fill the lungs, and then gently releasing it. This practice brings attention away from the swirling thoughts of the mind and anchors it in the present. Whether through meditation, mindful walking, or even mindful eating, this practice helps in reducing the intensity of anxiety and can provide a much-needed respite from the relentless chatter of a troubled mind.

Another valuable technique is cognitive restructuring. This involves identifying and challenging the negative thought patterns that often accompany depression and anxiety. By recognizing these thoughts for what they are —distortions of reality , —one can begin to replace them with more balanced perspectives. For instance, the thought "I am worthless" can be challenged with evidence of one's achievements and strengths. This process requires patience and practice but can significantly alter the way one interacts with their own mind.

Physical activity is another powerful tool in resisting the grip of these emotions. Exercise releases endorphins, the body's natural mood lifters, and can provide a sense of accomplishment and control. It doesn't have to be intense; even a short walk can make a difference. The rhythm of movement can be soothing, and being outdoors can offer a change of scenery that helps to shift one's mental state.

Connection with others is another vital technique. Isolation often exacerbates feelings of depression and anxiety, making it crucial to reach out to friends, family, or support groups. Sharing one's struggles with someone who listens without judgment can be incredibly healing. It reminds one that they are not alone, that their experiences are valid, and that there is hope in human connection. Sometimes, just knowing that someone else is there can be a lifeline.

Creative expression provides another avenue for resistance. Engaging in activities like writing, painting, or playing music allows one to process and express emotions in a non-verbal way. These activities can serve as an outlet for feelings that are difficult to articulate and can bring a sense of relief and accomplishment.

Finally, establishing a routine can provide a sense of stability and normalcy. Simple daily rituals, such as making the bed, preparing meals, or setting aside time for relaxation, can create a framework within which one can function more effectively. These routines can act as anchors, providing small achievements that contribute to a larger sense of order and predictability.

These techniques are not quick fixes; they require ongoing effort and commitment. They are tools to be used in conjunction with professional help, such as therapy or medication, when needed. The goal is not to eliminate grief, anxiety, or depression but to manage them in a way that allows for a more balanced and fulfilling life. Through mindfulness, cognitive restructuring, physical activity, connection, creative expression, and routine, one can begin to find moments of peace amidst the storm.

Affirmations for Self-Acceptance

Within the labyrinth of grief, anxiety, and depression, there exists an essential practice that serves as a gentle guide towards inner peace: the use of affirmations for self-acceptance. These affirmations act as beacons, illuminating the path through the dense fog of emotional turmoil. They offer a way to reconnect with oneself, to acknowledge and honor the person who exists beneath the layers of pain and confusion.

Affirmations are not mere words; they are powerful declarations that, when repeated with intention and belief, can reshape our inner dialogue. This inner dialogue often becomes tainted by the weight of grief and the shadows of anxiety and depression. Negative self-talk can be relentless, convincing us that we are unworthy, flawed, or incapable of overcoming our struggles. Affirmations counteract this negativity, planting seeds of self-compassion and acceptance.

The process of integrating affirmations into daily life begins with selecting phrases that resonate deeply. These statements should reflect truths that one aspires to internalize. For instance, "I am worthy of love and respect," or "I accept myself as I am, with all my strengths and imperfections." The choice of words is deeply personal, tailored to address the specific wounds and insecurities that one harbors.

Repetition is key. The practice of affirmations requires consistency and patience. It involves more than just reciting words; it demands that one speaks with conviction and feels the meaning behind each statement. This can be challenging, especially when the mind is clouded by self-doubt. However, with persistence, these affirmations begin to penetrate the subconscious, gradually transforming the way one perceives oneself.

Visualization can enhance the effectiveness of affirmations. As one speaks these positive declarations, envisioning a version of oneself that embodies these truths can create a powerful synergy. This mental imagery reinforces the affirmations, making them more tangible and believable. Over time, this practice can shift the internal landscape, fostering a sense of self-acceptance and inner harmony.

Incorporating affirmations into a daily routine can be a deeply grounding ritual. Whether it's starting the day with a few moments of mindful affirmation or ending the day with a reflection on these positive statements, this practice can serve as an anchor. It offers a moment of stillness and self-connection amidst the chaos of emotional upheaval.

The journey towards self-acceptance is not linear. There will be days when affirmations feel hollow, when the weight of grief, anxiety, or depression seems insurmountable. On these days, it is crucial to be gentle with oneself, to recognize that healing is a gradual process. The power of affirmations lies in their ability to provide a steady, unwavering source of support, even in the darkest times.

Affirmations for self-acceptance are a testament to the resilience of the human spirit. They remind us that, despite the challenges we face, we possess an innate worthiness and a capacity for self-love. By embracing this practice, we cultivate a compassionate inner voice, one that nurtures and sustains us through the trials of life. In the midst of grief, anxiety, and depression, affirmations offer a glimmer of hope, a reminder that self-acceptance is both possible and profoundly healing.

Overcoming Self-Judgment

Self-judgment often feels like a relentless critic that lives inside our minds, whispering doubts and harsh words when we are at our most vulnerable. It can become especially pronounced during periods of grief, anxiety, and depression. The weight of self-criticism can compound the already overwhelming emotions, making it difficult to navigate through the storm of feelings.

Understanding the origins of self-judgment is a crucial step. Many of us have internalized critical voices from our past—whether from parents, teachers, or peers. These voices can become ingrained, influencing how we perceive ourselves and our worth. Recognizing that these judgments are not inherent truths but learned behaviors can be liberating. It allows us to start questioning their validity and begin the process of unlearning.

One effective way to address self-judgment is through self-compassion. This involves treating ourselves with the same kindness and understanding that we would offer to a friend in a similar situation. It might feel unnatural at first, especially if we have spent years being hard on ourselves. However, practicing self-compassion can gradually soften the harsh inner dialogue. Simple acts like acknowledging our pain, reminding ourselves that suffering is a universal human experience, and offering ourselves gentle words of encouragement can make a significant difference.

Mindfulness also plays a vital role in overcoming self-judgment. By staying present and observing our thoughts without attachment, we can create a space between ourselves and our judgments. This detachment allows us to see these thoughts for what they are—fleeting and not necessarily reflective of reality. Mindfulness can be cultivated through meditation, deep breathing exercises, or simply paying attention to our daily activities with a non-judgmental attitude.

It is also important to challenge the negative beliefs we hold about ourselves. Cognitive-behavioral techniques can be useful here. This involves identifying negative thought patterns and actively disputing them with evidence and rational counter-arguments. For instance, if we find ourselves thinking, "I am a failure", we can counter this by listing our achievements, however small they may seem. This practice helps to rewire our thinking and gradually reduce the intensity of self-judgment.

Seeking support from others can provide a different perspective and offer validation. Sharing our struggles with trusted friends, family members, or a therapist can help us see ourselves through their compassionate eyes. Sometimes, an external viewpoint can illuminate strengths and qualities that we overlook or undervalue in ourselves. It is a reminder that we are not alone in our experiences and that others see worth and value in us, even when we struggle to see it ourselves.

Engaging in activities that foster a sense of accomplishment and joy can also mitigate self-judgment. Whether it's a hobby, a creative pursuit, or volunteering, these activities can help us reconnect with our sense of purpose and self-worth. They provide tangible evidence of our capabilities and remind us that we are more than our struggles.

In the face of grief, anxiety, and depression, self-judgment can feel like an additional burden. However, by understanding its origins, practicing self-compassion, cultivating mindfulness, challenging negative beliefs, seeking support, and engaging in fulfilling activities, we can begin to alleviate its weight. This journey is not about eradicating self-judgment entirely but about learning to navigate it with greater ease and resilience.

Chapter 8: The Earthly Journey

Challenges We Face

Navigating the turbulent waters of grief, anxiety, and depression often feels like being adrift in a storm without a compass. Each wave that crashes over us brings a new challenge, a fresh obstacle that tests our resilience and resolve. These experiences, though deeply personal, are universally felt, touching every corner of our lives and reshaping our perceptions.

Grief, in its many forms, is a profound and often misunderstood emotion. It is not simply the sorrow we feel after a loss, but a complex tapestry of emotions that can include anger, guilt, confusion, and even relief. The challenge lies in its unpredictability; it can strike at any moment, triggered by a memory, a scent, a song. It does not follow a linear path and does not adhere to any timetable. This can leave us feeling unprepared and overwhelmed, struggling to find a way to cope with the void that has been left behind.

Anxiety, on the other hand, is a relentless companion that shadows us, turning the mundane into the insurmountable. It manifests as a constant state of worry, a gnawing sense of dread that something terrible is about to happen. This can be exhausting, draining our energy and leaving us in a perpetual state of hyper-vigilance. The challenge here is not just the anxiety itself, but the way it isolates us, making it difficult to reach out for support or even to articulate what we are feeling. It can distort our reality, making us question our worth and our ability to cope with life's demands.

Depression, often described as a black hole, is a profound and pervasive sense of hopelessness and despair. It saps the joy from our lives and leaves us feeling empty and disconnected. The challenge of depression is its insidious nature; it creeps in slowly, often unnoticed until it has taken a firm hold. It can rob us of our motivation, our ability to find pleasure in the things we once loved, and can make even the simplest tasks feel like monumental efforts. It is not just a state of mind but a profound alteration of our entire being, affecting our thoughts, our behaviors, and our physical health.

These challenges are compounded by the stigma that still surrounds mental health issues. Society often views grief, anxiety, and depression as weaknesses, something to be hidden or ashamed of. This can prevent us from seeking the help we need, from talking openly about our experiences, and from finding the support that is so crucial to our healing. The silence that surrounds these issues can be as damaging as the conditions themselves, perpetuating a cycle of isolation and suffering.

Understanding these challenges is the first step towards overcoming them. It requires a willingness to confront our emotions, to acknowledge our struggles, and to seek out the support and resources that can help us navigate this difficult terrain. It is a journey that requires patience, compassion, and a deep commitment to our own well-being. By facing these challenges head-on, we can begin to find our way through the darkness and towards a place of healing and hope.

Growth Through Experiences

Navigating the turbulent waters of grief, anxiety, and depression often feels like being caught in a relentless storm. Yet, it is within these very storms that we find the opportunity for profound growth and transformation. Our experiences, no matter how painful or challenging, carry within them the seeds of resilience and wisdom.

Reflecting on my own encounters with grief, I remember the overwhelming sense of loss and the suffocating weight of sorrow. The days blurred into nights, and the future seemed an insurmountable mountain. Initially, I resisted the pain, trying to numb it with distractions and denial. But as time passed, I realized that avoiding my feelings only deepened my suffering. It was only when I allowed myself to fully experience my grief that I began to heal.

Anxiety, too, has been a relentless companion at times. The constant worry and fear of the unknown often paralyzed me, making even the simplest tasks feel daunting. However, through therapy and mindfulness practices, I learned to recognize the triggers of my anxiety and develop coping strategies. By facing my fears head-on and understanding their roots, I discovered a strength within myself that I never knew existed.

Depression, with its heavy cloak of darkness, has taught me the importance of self-compassion. During my deepest bouts of depression, I often felt worthless and isolated. It was easy to fall into the trap of self-criticism and hopelessness. But through the support of loved ones and professional guidance, I learned to treat myself with kindness and patience. Each small step forward, no matter how insignificant it seemed, was a victory worth celebrating.

One of the most valuable lessons I've learned through these experiences is the importance of connection. Sharing my struggles with others who have faced similar challenges has been incredibly healing. In these shared moments of vulnerability, we find solidarity and understanding. It reminds us that we are not alone, and that our feelings, no matter how intense, are valid.

Another key insight has been the realization that growth is not linear. There are days when progress feels tangible and other days when setbacks seem to erase all forward movement. Accepting this ebb and flow has been crucial in maintaining hope and perseverance. It's in these moments of regression that we often learn the most about ourselves and our capacity for resilience.

Reflecting on my journey, I've come to appreciate the beauty of imperfection. Life's challenges have a way of stripping us down to our core, revealing our vulnerabilities and strengths in equal measure. It's through these raw and unfiltered experiences that we truly come to understand ourselves and our place in the world.

Our struggles with grief, anxiety, and depression are not just battles to be fought, but opportunities for growth and self-discovery. Each experience, no matter how painful, contributes to our evolution as individuals. By facing our emotions head-on and seeking support when needed, we pave the way for a deeper understanding of ourselves and a more compassionate outlook on life. Through these experiences, we learn that even in our darkest moments, there is potential for light and growth.

Understanding Our Choices

When faced with grief, anxiety, and depression, it becomes evident that our responses and coping mechanisms play a crucial role in shaping our experiences. Choices, often subtle and seemingly insignificant, accumulate to create a path through the darkness or lead us further into it. Reflecting on these choices allows us to understand their profound impact on our mental and emotional well-being.

In the midst of grief, the initial shock can cloud our judgment, making it difficult to see the options available to us. Yet, even in this haze, every small decision matters. Do we seek support from friends and family, or do we isolate ourselves, believing that no one can truly understand our pain? Choosing to reach out, even when it feels impossible, can be a lifeline, offering a sense of connection and shared humanity.

Anxiety, with its relentless grip, often convinces us that we have no control over our circumstances. However, recognizing that we can choose our reactions to anxiety-inducing situations is empowering. We might decide to confront our fears gradually, taking small steps toward what scares us, or we might opt for avoidance, which often leads to a cycle of increased anxiety. Each choice, however small, can either reinforce our fears or help dismantle them.

Depression, perhaps the most insidious of the three, often strips away our motivation to make any choices at all. The weight of hopelessness can make the simplest decisions feel monumental. Yet, in these moments, choosing self-compassion over self-criticism can make a world of difference. Allowing ourselves to acknowledge our struggles without judgment, and to take even the smallest steps toward self-care, can slowly begin to lift the fog.

Understanding our choices also involves recognizing the influence of external factors. Societal expectations, cultural norms, and the opinions of those around us can shape our decisions in ways we might not immediately realize. Reflecting on these influences helps us discern whether our choices are truly our own or if they are being unduly swayed by external pressures.

Moreover, it's essential to recognize that our choices are not always linear or consistent. There will be days when we make strides toward healing and other days when taking any step feels impossible. This ebb and flow are natural, and understanding this can prevent us from falling into the trap of self-blame during setbacks.

Therapeutic interventions, mindfulness practices, and support groups offer structured ways to explore and understand our choices. These resources provide tools and strategies to navigate our emotions and make informed decisions that align with our values and well-being. However, the first step often involves acknowledging that we have choices, even when it feels like we don't.

Reflecting on our choices in the context of grief, anxiety, and depression reveals the power we hold in shaping our journey. Each decision, no matter how small, contributes to our overall well-being. By understanding and consciously making choices that support our healing, we can gradually find our way through the darkness and into a place of greater peace and resilience.

Aligning with Purpose

In the turbulent waves of grief, anxiety, and depression, the notion of aligning with purpose can seem distant, almost unattainable. Yet, it is within this very alignment that we often find the most profound sense of solace. Purpose, in its essence, is not just a grandiose life mission but a series of small, meaningful actions that tether us to the present and provide a beacon of hope amidst the darkness.

Reflecting on one's purpose requires a deep dive into personal values and beliefs. It is about understanding what drives us, what we hold dear, and how these can serve as anchors in moments of despair.

For many, this involves a reevaluation of priorities and a shift in perspective. When life feels overwhelming, reconnecting with these core values can offer a renewed sense of direction and clarity.

Purpose does not necessarily eliminate the pain of grief or the heaviness of depression, but it provides a lens through which these experiences can be viewed differently. It transforms suffering into a part of a larger narrative, one that is not defined by the pain alone but by the resilience and growth that emerge from it. This shift in perspective can be empowering, allowing individuals to see themselves not just as victims of their circumstances, but as active participants in their own healing journey.

Engaging in activities that align with one's purpose can also serve as a practical tool for managing anxiety and depression. Whether it is through volunteering, creative expression, or simply being present for loved ones, these actions foster a sense of fulfillment and connection. They remind us that our lives have meaning and that we can contribute positively to the world around us.

Purpose is not static; it evolves with us. What may have been a source of motivation in the past might change as we grow and our circumstances shift. It is important to remain open to this evolution, to allow our purpose to adapt and transform in alignment with our current state of being. This flexibility can prevent feelings of stagnation and help us navigate the complexities of our emotional landscapes.

In seeking purpose, it is also crucial to acknowledge the small victories and moments of joy that punctuate our days. These seemingly minor instances are often the building blocks of a purposeful life. They remind us that purpose is not solely found in monumental achievements but in the everyday acts of kindness, creativity, and connection that enrich our existence.

It is essential to approach the concept of purpose with compassion and patience. There is no right or wrong way to find it, and the path may be fraught with setbacks and uncertainties. However, each step taken in alignment with our values brings us closer to a life that feels authentic and meaningful.

In the end, aligning with purpose is about finding a sense of coherence in the chaos, a thread that weaves through our experiences and binds them into a tapestry of meaning. It is about recognizing that even in the throes of grief, anxiety, and depression, we have the capacity to create a life of purpose and significance.

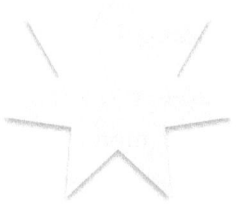

Chapter 9: Energy Connections

The Energy Level Connection

Reflecting on the intricate dance of emotions, one often finds that grief, anxiety, and depression are interwoven in ways that are both subtle and profound. These emotional states, though distinct, share a common thread that binds them together: the energy level connection. This connection is not just about the physical energy we expend but also about the emotional and mental energy that fuels our daily existence.

When faced with grief, the energy one normally reserves for daily tasks seems to dissipate. The weight of loss can be overwhelming, draining the vitality that once seemed boundless. It becomes a challenge to muster the strength to face the simplest of activities. This depletion of energy is not merely physical; it is deeply emotional. The heart feels heavy, and the mind becomes clouded with memories and what-ifs. This profound sorrow can manifest in a physical sense, making it difficult to differentiate between emotional fatigue and physical exhaustion.

Anxiety, on the other hand, operates on a different frequency. It is an energy that is often frantic and scattered. The mind races with thoughts of the future, potential dangers, and the unknown. This constant state of alertness can be exhausting. The body is in a perpetual state of readiness, muscles tense, and the heart often races. The energy consumed by anxiety is relentless, leaving little room for relaxation or peace. It's as if the mind is a hamster on a wheel, constantly turning but never getting anywhere. This ceaseless motion drains one's reserves, leaving a person feeling worn out and frazzled.

Depression, meanwhile, is often characterized by a profound lack of energy. It is a state of inertia, where even the simplest tasks seem insurmountable. The energy that once fueled passions and interests is conspicuously absent. There is a pervasive sense of emptiness and a heavy fog that dulls the senses. The world appears colorless, and the motivation to engage with it diminishes. This lack of energy is not just a symptom but a defining feature of depression. It is as if the spark that once lit the fire within has been extinguished, leaving only cold ashes.

Understanding the energy level connection between these emotional states can offer insights into their management and healing. Recognizing that grief, anxiety, and depression affect our energy in different ways can help us tailor our approaches to self-care. For instance, while physical rest might be crucial for someone in the throes of grief, someone grappling with anxiety might benefit more from techniques that calm the mind and reduce the frantic energy. Similarly, those dealing with depression might need strategies to gently rekindle their energy and motivation.

Reflecting on these connections also fosters empathy. When we see someone struggling with grief, anxiety, or depression, understanding the energy dynamics at play can help us offer more compassionate support. We realize that their struggle is not just emotional but also deeply physical. Their energy reserves are being taxed in ways that might not be immediately visible.

In the end, the energy level connection serves as a reminder of the holistic nature of our well-being. Our emotional states are not isolated experiences but are deeply intertwined with our physical and mental energy. By acknowledging and addressing this connection, we can better navigate the complex landscape of grief, anxiety, and depression, finding pathways to healing that honor the full spectrum of our human experience.

Soul-Level Choices

Navigating through the labyrinth of grief, anxiety, and depression often feels like an unending night. Each twist and turn can seem overwhelming, but there lies a profound truth beneath these emotional waves. At the core of our being, we make choices that resonate on a soul level, choices that shape our paths and define our healing journey.

In the quiet moments of reflection, it becomes evident that our responses to life's trials are not merely reactive. They are, in many ways, the echoes of our deepest values and beliefs. When faced with loss, the immediate instinct might be to retreat into ourselves, to shield our hearts from further pain. Yet, within this self-imposed cocoon, a more significant decision is brewing. Do we allow this grief to consume us, or do we seek a deeper understanding of our pain?

Anxiety, with its relentless grip, often feels like a storm raging within. It's easy to view it as an unwelcome intruder, an enemy to be vanquished. However, beneath its tumultuous surface lies a message, a call from our inner self to pay attention. This is where the soul-level choice becomes paramount. Do we suppress this anxiety, pushing it into the recesses of our mind, OR do we listen to it, understand it as a signal that something in our life requires attention?

Depression, often described as a heavy fog, can obscure our vision and make the world seem devoid of color. It whispers of hopelessness and despair, urging us to give in to its weight. Yet, even in these darkest moments, there is a flicker of choice. This choice is not about denying the existence of depression but about how we engage with it. Do we let it define us, or do we seek to uncover the lessons it holds? This decision, though deeply personal, can be transformative. It speaks to our resilience, our capacity to find meaning even in the midst of suffering.

These choices are not made in isolation but are a consequence of what we have learnt and evolved through, during the course of multiple life-times. They are influenced by our past experiences, our cultural backgrounds, and our support systems. They are shaped by the stories we tell ourselves and the narratives we believe about the world. Acknowledging this interconnectedness can be empowering. It reminds us that while we may feel alone in our struggles, we are part of a larger tapestry of human experience.

It's important to recognize that these choices are not about quick fixes or easy solutions. They are about a shift in perspective, a willingness to look within and confront the truths that lie there. This process requires patience, self-compassion, and a commitment to growth. It is about honoring our pain and allowing it to guide us towards healing.

In the end, these soul-level choices are about reclaiming our power. They are about understanding that while we may not have control over the events that befall us, we do have control over how we respond. This realization can be a beacon of light in the darkness, a reminder that within us lies the strength to navigate even the most challenging of emotional landscapes.

Purpose of Meeting Others

Connecting with others during times of grief, anxiety, and depression can feel like a daunting task. The weight of our emotions often makes us retreat within ourselves, seeking solace in solitude. Yet, the act of reaching out to others holds profound significance. It is not merely about seeking comfort but about finding a shared human experience that can offer a different perspective on our own struggles.

When we interact with others, we often discover that we are not as alone in our feelings as we might have thought. The realization that someone else has traversed a similar path can be incredibly validating. It helps to normalize our emotions, making them feel less overwhelming and isolating. There is a certain kind of healing that takes place when someone says "I understand" and truly means it. This shared understanding does not erase the pain but does make it more bearable.

Meeting others also provides an opportunity for us to express our emotions in a safe space. Verbalizing our thoughts and feelings can be therapeutic. It allows us to process our grief, anxiety, and depression in a way that internal contemplation often cannot. The act of speaking about our experiences forces us to organize our thoughts and confront our emotions head-on. This can lead to moments of clarity and insight that might not have been possible in isolation.

Furthermore, the support we receive from others can come in many forms. Sometimes it is a listening ear, other times it is practical assistance or encouraging words. The kindness of others can act as a reminder of the goodness that still exists in the world, even when our own outlook is bleak. These small acts of kindness can accumulate, gradually lifting the weight of our burdens.

Interaction with others also opens the door to new coping strategies. Different people have different ways of dealing with grief, anxiety, and depression. By engaging with others, we expose ourselves to a variety of coping mechanisms that we might not have considered on our own. This exchange of ideas can be incredibly beneficial, providing us with tools that can help us navigate our own emotional landscape more effectively.

However, it is important to acknowledge that not all interactions will be positive. There will be moments when well-meaning individuals say the wrong thing or fail to understand the depth of our pain. These experiences can be hurtful, but they are also part of the process. They teach us about resilience and the importance of setting boundaries. Knowing when to distance ourselves from unhelpful interactions is just as crucial as seeking out supportive ones.

Amid grief, anxiety, and depression, it is easy to underestimate the importance of social connections. The tendency to withdraw is strong, but the benefits of meeting others can be profound. It is through these interactions that we can find validation, express our emotions, receive support, and discover new coping mechanisms. Despite the challenges, the effort to connect with others is often rewarded with a sense of shared humanity and emotional relief that can be pivotal in our healing process.

The Role of Coincidence

Coincidences often appear as curious anomalies in the tapestry of life, seemingly random threads woven into our experiences. They can be a source of wonder, confusion, and even solace. When dealing with grief, anxiety, and depression, these unexpected events can take on profound significance, challenging our understanding of causality and control.

In moments of profound loss or intense emotional turmoil, the mind is desperate for meaning. It clings to patterns, searching for signs that there is order amidst the chaos. A chance encounter, a song on the radio, or a familiar smell can feel like more than mere happenstance. These occurrences can be interpreted as messages, whether from a higher power, the universe, or our own subconscious minds. They can serve as reminders that we are not alone, that there is some unseen connection guiding us through our pain.

It is not uncommon for someone grieving to notice a series of events that seem too perfectly timed to be accidental. Perhaps a loved one's favorite flower blooms unexpectedly, or a long-lost friend reaches out just when needed most. These moments can offer a glimmer of hope, a fleeting sense that there is purpose in the suffering. For those battling anxiety, coincidences might appear as validations of their fears or, conversely, as reassurances that their worries are unfounded. The unpredictable nature of anxiety often makes any semblance of control feel like a lifeline.

Depression, with its heavy fog of despair and hopelessness, can make it difficult to see any light. Coincidences in such a state may be met with skepticism or indifference, yet they can also provide small sparks of curiosity or wonder. A serendipitous event might briefly pierce the veil, offering a momentary distraction from the weight of sadness. These instances can be precious, even if fleeting, as they remind those suffering that the world still holds surprises, that life is not entirely devoid of spontaneity and magic.

However, it is crucial to approach the interpretation of coincidences with a balanced perspective. While they can provide comfort and a sense of connection, they should not be relied upon as definitive answers or solutions. The human mind has a tendency to seek patterns, sometimes seeing connections where none exist. This can lead to an overreliance on the mystical, potentially distracting from the tangible steps needed to address grief, anxiety, and depression.

Reflecting on coincidences can also lead to a deeper understanding of our own minds and emotions. Why do certain events stand out to us? What do they reveal about our hopes, fears, and desires? By examining these questions, we can gain insight into our internal landscapes, fostering greater self-awareness and emotional resilience.

Coincidences, in their mysterious and unpredictable nature, challenge us to remain open to the unknown. They remind us that not everything can be planned or controlled, and that there is beauty in the unexpected. For those navigating the difficult terrain of grief, anxiety, and depression, these moments can serve as gentle nudges towards healing, encouraging a sense of curiosity and wonder about the world and our place within it.

Chapter 10: Aligning with Universal Truth

Helping Each Other

In the midst of grief, anxiety, and depression, the act of coming together and supporting one another can be a lifeline. The power of human connection becomes a beacon of hope in the darkest of times. Reflecting on this, I am reminded of the many ways in which we, as individuals, can make a significant difference in each other's lives.

The first step often begins with recognizing that we are not alone. The feeling of isolation can be overwhelming, but reaching out to someone who understands can provide immense relief. Sharing experiences and emotions openly can foster a sense of belonging and mutual understanding. When we listen without judgment, we offer a safe space for others to express their pain, fears, and uncertainties. This act of listening is not passive; it is a powerful form of support that validates the other person's feelings and experiences.

In helping each other, empathy plays a crucial role. Empathy is more than just understanding; it is about feeling with the other person. It involves putting ourselves in their shoes and seeing the world through their eyes. This deep connection can bridge the gap between individuals, creating a sense of solidarity and shared humanity. When we show empathy, we communicate that the other person's feelings are important and that they matter.

Practical support is equally important. Sometimes, words are not enough, and actions speak louder. Offering to help with daily tasks, providing a meal, or simply being present can alleviate some of the burdens that come with grief, anxiety, and depression. These gestures, though seemingly small, can have a profound impact on someone's well-being. They remind the person that they are cared for and that they do not have to navigate their struggles alone.

It is also essential to encourage professional help when needed. While peer support is invaluable, there are times when the expertise of a mental health professional is necessary. Gently guiding someone towards seeking therapy or counseling can be a crucial step in their healing process. It is important to approach this suggestion with sensitivity, ensuring that the person feels supported rather than pressured.

Creating a supportive environment involves being mindful of our own limitations as well. Helping others should not come at the expense of our own mental health. It is vital to recognize when we need to step back and take care of ourselves. Setting boundaries and practicing self-care allows us to maintain our own well-being while being there for others. This balance ensures that we can continue to offer genuine support without burning out.

Reflecting on these aspects of helping each other, it becomes clear that support is a two-way street. It is about giving and receiving, about mutual respect and understanding. When we come together in times of grief, anxiety, and depression, we create a network of care that strengthens us all. This collective effort can transform the way we experience and cope with our struggles, making the journey a little less daunting and a lot more hopeful.

Serving a Larger Purpose

Reflecting on the depths of grief, anxiety, and depression, I have often found myself questioning the larger purpose behind such overwhelming emotions. It is in the quiet moments, when the world seems too heavy and the silence too loud, that one begins to ponder the reason behind such suffering. What if these emotions serve a greater role in our lives, pushing us towards growth and understanding?

At first glance, grief might appear as a dark, endless tunnel. It is the shadow that lingers after the loss of a loved one, the sorrow that grips the heart and refuses to let go. Yet, within this sorrow lies a profound lesson about the value of relationships and the impermanence of life. Grief compels us to cherish the moments we have, to express love freely, and to acknowledge the transient nature of our existence. Through grief, we learn to honor those we have lost by living more fully and loving more deeply.

Anxiety, often seen as a relentless intruder, has its own role to play. It is the mind's way of alerting us to potential threats, real or imagined. While it can be paralyzing and exhausting, anxiety can also be a catalyst for change. It forces us to confront our fears, to prepare for challenges, and to develop resilience. By facing anxiety head-on, we gain a deeper understanding of our triggers and learn strategies to manage our responses. This process, though arduous, fosters personal growth and equips us with tools to navigate future uncertainties.

Depression, with its heavy cloak of despair, might seem devoid of any purpose. It drains color from life, leaving a monochrome existence where joy feels unattainable. However, depression can also be a signal that something in our lives is out of balance. It urges us to look inward, to reassess our values, and to seek out what truly brings fulfillment. In the depths of depression, there lies an opportunity for profound self-discovery. By seeking help, whether through therapy, medication, or support networks, we begin to rebuild our lives with a clearer sense of purpose and direction.

These emotions, though painful, are not without meaning. They challenge us to grow, to adapt, and to find strength within ourselves. They remind us of our humanity, our capacity for empathy, and our need for connection. By serving a larger purpose, grief, anxiety, and depression become more than just burdens; they become catalysts for transformation.

In the process of reflecting on these emotions, one can find a sense of purpose that transcends the pain. It is not about erasing the emotions or pretending they do not exist, but about integrating them into our lives in a way that fosters growth. By acknowledging the lessons they bring, we can transform our suffering into a source of strength and wisdom.

Each person's experience with these emotions is unique, yet the underlying themes of growth, understanding, and resilience remain constant. In recognizing the larger purpose behind our struggles, we can begin to navigate the complexities of grief, anxiety, and depression with a renewed sense of hope and determination. Through reflection, we find that even in the darkest moments, there is potential for light and transformation.

Aligning with Truth

Understanding the essence of our own truth is a profound step in navigating the turbulent waters of grief, anxiety, and depression. Often, in the midst of our struggles, we find ourselves distanced from our core beliefs and values. This disconnection can amplify our sense of loss and confusion, making it even harder to find our way back to a place of peace and clarity.

Reflecting on one's truth requires a willingness to look inward with honesty and compassion. It is about peeling back the layers of societal expectations, past traumas, and self-imposed limitations to discover what genuinely resonates within us. This process is neither quick nor easy, but it is essential for healing. By aligning with our truth, we begin to foster a sense of authenticity that can anchor us amidst the chaos.

One effective method to start this alignment is through mindful self-inquiry. Sitting quietly with our thoughts, we can ask ourselves probing questions: What are my deepest values? What beliefs have I adopted that no longer serve me? How do I truly feel about my current situation? Allowing these questions to surface without judgment can reveal insights that have been buried under layers of pain and fear.

As we start to uncover our truth, it is important to practice self-compassion. The journey can bring to light uncomfortable realizations and past mistakes. Instead of criticizing ourselves for these revelations, we can choose to view them as opportunities for growth. Embracing our imperfections and vulnerabilities is a crucial part of aligning with our truth. It is through acknowledging and accepting these parts of ourselves that we can begin to heal more fully.

Another vital aspect of this alignment is the recognition of our own needs and boundaries. In times of grief, anxiety, and depression, it is common to lose sight of what we need to feel safe and supported. Reconnecting with our truth involves understanding and respecting our limits. Whether it means taking time for solitude, seeking professional help, or setting boundaries with others, honoring our needs is a powerful act of self-respect.

Community also plays a significant role in this process. Sharing our journey with trusted friends, family, or support groups can provide a mirror to our truth. These connections offer validation and different perspectives that can help us see ourselves more clearly. It is through these interactions that we can find the courage to stand in our truth, even when it feels uncomfortable.

Patience is another key element. Aligning with our truth is not a linear path but a continuous unfolding. There will be setbacks and moments of doubt, but each step taken with intention brings us closer to a more authentic existence. It is a dynamic process that evolves as we grow and change.

In essence, aligning with our truth is about living in a way that is congruent with who we truly are. It is a commitment to ourselves, a promise to honor our deepest values and beliefs. This alignment does not eliminate the pain of grief, anxiety, or depression, but it provides a foundation of authenticity and strength that can support us through these challenges. By staying true to ourselves, we build resilience and find a path to healing that is uniquely our own.

Connecting with Divinity

In the midst of life's most challenging moments, when grief, anxiety, and depression seem to engulf the soul, there lies an often overlooked sanctuary within us—a connection to the divine. It's a space where solace and understanding reside, offering a profound sense of peace that transcends the turmoil of our emotions.

The path to this sacred connection isn't always clear or straightforward. It requires a willingness to look beyond the immediate pain and seek something greater than ourselves. For some, this might mean turning to religious practices, engaging in prayer, or participating in rituals that have been passed down through generations. For others, it could be found in the quiet moments of meditation, where the mind is stilled, and the heart is open to receive whatever wisdom or comfort the universe has to offer.

In these practices, there is a subtle yet powerful shift that occurs. The act of reaching out to a higher power, whatever form that may take, allows us to step outside of our own suffering. It provides a perspective that is both humbling and empowering. We begin to see that our pain, while deeply personal, is also a part of the broader human experience. This realization can be incredibly freeing, as it reminds us that we are not alone in our struggles.

Moreover, connecting with divinity can offer a sense of purpose and meaning that is often lost in the throes of grief and depression. It can be a reminder that life, despite its hardships, holds a deeper significance. This connection can illuminate the path forward, showing us that even in our darkest times, there is light to be found. It encourages us to trust in the process of healing, to have faith that we are being guided towards a better place, even if we cannot see it yet.

It's important to acknowledge that this connection doesn't always come easily. There may be moments of doubt, frustration, and even anger. These emotions are natural and valid. Spiritual connection is not about bypassing these feelings but rather about acknowledging them and allowing the divine to help us navigate through them. It's a relationship that requires patience, openness, and a willingness to be vulnerable.

In this sacred space, we can also find a sense of community. Whether through a faith group, a meditation circle, or simply sharing our experiences with like-minded individuals, there is strength in knowing that others are walking a similar path. This communal aspect of spirituality can provide additional support and encouragement, reinforcing the idea that we are all interconnected.

As we continue to explore and deepen our connection with divinity, we may begin to notice subtle changes within ourselves. There might be a growing sense of inner peace, a newfound resilience, or an increased capacity for compassion towards ourselves and others. These shifts, while sometimes imperceptible, are significant markers of our healing journey.

In essence, the divine connection is a powerful tool in navigating the complexities of grief, anxiety, and depression. It offers a sanctuary for the soul, a place where we can find solace, understanding, and a renewed sense of hope. Through this connection, we can begin to heal, to transform our pain into something meaningful, and to move forward with a greater sense of purpose and peace.

Chapter 11: Dealing with Life Situations

Tormenting Situations

The weight of grief can be an all-encompassing presence, one that seeps into every corner of existence, altering perceptions and distorting realities. It's often in the quiet moments, when the world is still, that the magnitude of loss reveals itself most profoundly. The silence becomes deafening, amplifying the void left behind by a loved one. In these moments, the mind races, replaying memories like a broken record, each loop a reminder of what once was and what can never be again.

Anxiety, on the other hand, has a way of creeping in, uninvited and persistent. It's the unrelenting sense of impending doom, the feeling that something terrible is lurking just around the corner. It manifests in various ways—sweaty palms, a racing heart, or a mind that won't quiet down. The body remains on high alert, muscles tense, as if preparing for a battle that never quite materializes. This constant state of vigilance is exhausting, leaving one drained and yet unable to find peace.

Depression casts a long, dark shadow over daily life, sapping energy and motivation. It's not merely sadness, but a profound sense of emptiness and hopelessness. Getting out of bed feels like an insurmountable task, and even the simplest of activities seem overwhelming. The world appears in shades of gray, colors muted by the heavy fog of despair. There's a sense of disconnection from others, an invisible barrier that isolates and alienates. It's as if the mind is trapped in a cage, with no discernible way out.

These tormenting situations often overlap, creating a tangled web of emotional and psychological turmoil. Grief may trigger anxiety, as the loss of a loved one brings uncertainty about the future. Anxiety can lead to depression, as the constant state of fear and worry erodes one's sense of well-being. Depression, in turn, can deepen the sense of grief, making it harder to move forward and find meaning in life again. It's a vicious cycle, each condition feeding into the other, compounding the overall distress.

The struggle to navigate these emotions can feel isolating, as if no one else could possibly understand the depth of the pain. There's a tendency to withdraw, to retreat into oneself, which only serves to intensify the feelings of loneliness and despair. Well-meaning advice from others often falls flat, as platitudes and clichés do little to alleviate the suffering. The journey through grief, anxiety, and depression is deeply personal, and what works for one person may not work for another.

Finding ways to cope with these tormenting situations requires patience and self-compassion. It's important to acknowledge the pain, to give oneself permission to feel and to grieve. Seeking support, whether through therapy, support groups, or trusted friends and family, can provide a lifeline, a reminder that one is not alone in this struggle. Small, incremental steps can make a difference, gradually building resilience and strength.

In these moments of darkness, it's crucial to hold on to the belief that there is light at the end of the tunnel. The process of healing is not linear, and setbacks are a natural part of the journey. Each day is a new opportunity to find moments of peace and to reclaim a sense of hope and purpose.

Painful Journeys

Every step taken during times of grief, anxiety, and depression feels like traversing a landscape shrouded in mist. The familiar becomes alien, and the once-comforting corners of our minds turn into echo chambers of sorrow and despair. Each day presents a new challenge, a new hurdle that seems insurmountable. The weight of emotions can be overwhelming, making even the simplest tasks feel monumental.

In these moments, the world seems to shrink, and our vision narrows to a tunnel of pain. It's as if the walls are closing in, leaving little room for light or hope. The mind becomes a battleground, where every thought is a potential trigger, every memory a potential source of anguish. The struggle to maintain a semblance of normalcy becomes a daily endeavor, often leaving one feeling exhausted and defeated.

Yet, amidst the turmoil, there are fleeting moments of clarity. These moments, though rare, are precious. They offer a glimmer of understanding, a brief respite from the storm. It is during these times that one can begin to reflect on the nature of their suffering. The process of introspection, although painful, can be a crucial step toward healing. It allows for the acknowledgment of pain, the recognition of its source, and the beginning of a path toward acceptance.

The significance of self-awareness cannot be understated. Understanding the triggers and patterns that exacerbate feelings of grief, anxiety, and depression can provide a sense of control in an otherwise chaotic experience. It is through this awareness that one can start to develop coping mechanisms, small yet significant tools to navigate the emotional labyrinth.

There is a certain paradox in the experience of such profound emotions. On one hand, they isolate, creating a barrier between oneself and the rest of the world. On the other hand, they are a universal experience, something that connects us all on a deeply human level. This duality can be both comforting and disconcerting. Knowing that others have walked similar paths can offer solace, yet it also underscores the pervasive nature of suffering.

Finding ways to express these emotions is vital. Whether through writing, art, music, or conversation, the act of externalizing internal turmoil can be therapeutic. It transforms abstract feelings into tangible expressions, making them easier to understand and manage. Creative outlets serve as a bridge between the internal and external worlds, providing a means to communicate what words often fail to capture.

Support systems play an integral role during these times. Friends, family, therapists, and support groups can offer invaluable perspectives and encouragement. Their presence can serve as a reminder that one is not alone, that there are others who care and are willing to listen. The act of reaching out, though daunting, can be a lifeline.

The path through grief, anxiety, and depression is neither linear nor predictable. It is a deeply personal experience, shaped by individual circumstances and perspectives. Each person's experience is unique, yet there are common threads that bind us together. Acknowledging and accepting these emotions is not a sign of weakness, but rather a testament to our resilience and capacity for growth.

Moving forward requires patience and compassion, both for oneself and others. It is a journey of small steps, each one a testament to the human spirit's ability to endure and eventually find light in the darkest of times.

No Judgment from the Universe

Reflective style often involves a contemplative and introspective tone, focusing on personal insights, philosophical musings, and a deep connection with the reader's emotions. Here is the requested subchapter:

When grappling with grief, anxiety, and depression, it's easy to feel as though the universe has singled you out for suffering. The weight of these emotions can lead to a sense of isolation, as if you are being unfairly judged by some cosmic force. Yet, it is essential to understand that the universe operates without judgment. It is indifferent to our struggles, neither condemning nor exalting us.

The stars, the planets, the vast expanse of space – they exist in a state of neutrality. They do not assign value to our experiences or label our emotions as good or bad. This realization can be liberating. It offers a perspective that our pain is not a punishment, nor is our happiness a reward. The universe simply is, and within it, we are allowed to be.

In the throes of grief, there is often a tendency to search for meaning or reason. Why did this happen to me? What did I do to deserve this? These questions can spiral into a narrative of self-blame and perceived cosmic retribution. However, acknowledging that the universe does not judge can help us release these harmful patterns of thought. It allows us to see our experiences as part of a broader, impartial existence.

Similarly, anxiety often stems from a fear of being judged – by others, by ourselves, or by some higher power. The constant worry about how we are perceived can amplify our stress and hinder our ability to find peace. Understanding that the universe is indifferent to our perceived flaws can be a soothing balm. It encourages us to be kinder to ourselves, to recognize that our worth is not contingent upon the approval of an unfeeling cosmos.

Depression, with its pervasive sense of hopelessness, can make the world feel like a hostile place. The belief that we are being judged harshly for our shortcomings can deepen our despair. Yet, the realization that the universe does not judge us can offer a glimmer of solace. It suggests that our struggles are not a reflection of our value but rather a part of the human experience. We are not lesser beings because we suffer; we are simply beings who suffer.

This perspective does not diminish the reality of our emotions. Grief, anxiety, and depression are profound and valid experiences. However, understanding that the universe is neutral can help us navigate these emotions with a bit more compassion for ourselves. It can remind us that we are not alone in our suffering, even if the universe remains indifferent.

In this neutrality, there is a kind of freedom. We are free to feel without the burden of cosmic judgment. We are free to seek healing and growth without the fear of being deemed unworthy. The universe's indifference is not cold or uncaring; it is a vast, open space in which we are free to exist as we are.

By embracing this perspective, we can begin to release the weight of self-judgment. We can allow ourselves to grieve, to feel anxious, to be depressed, without adding the burden of perceived cosmic disapproval. In this way, we might find a path to healing that is gentler, more forgiving, and ultimately more human.

~

Reflective style is maintained throughout, focusing on introspection and philosophical musings to connect deeply with the reader's emotions.

Understanding Divinity Within

In the midst of sorrow, anxiety, and depression, there often lies a profound sense of disconnection—not just from others, but from our very selves. This disconnection can create a chasm, making it difficult to find meaning or solace in our experiences. Yet, within each of us, there exists a spark, a divine essence that can serve as a guiding light through the darkest of times.

Recognizing this inner divinity begins with stillness. It is in moments of quiet reflection that we can start to hear the faint whispers of our true nature. These whispers remind us that we are more than our grief, more than our anxiety, more than our depression. We are beings of infinite potential, capable of profound growth and transformation. This realization does not diminish the reality of our pain, but it can provide a new lens through which to view it.

Connecting with this inner divinity often involves a deep and compassionate self-examination. It requires us to look beyond the surface of our emotions and thoughts, to explore the underlying truths of our existence. This process can be both challenging and liberating. It asks us to confront our fears and insecurities, but it also invites us to acknowledge our strengths and virtues. Through this balanced introspection, we can begin to see ourselves not as flawed or broken, but as whole beings navigating the complexities of human experience.

One way to nurture this connection is through mindfulness practices. Whether it be meditation, prayer, or simply spending time in nature, these practices help us to center ourselves and cultivate an awareness of the present moment. In doing so, we create space for our inner divinity to emerge. We become more attuned to the subtle energies within and around us, and we start to recognize the interconnectedness of all things. This awareness can bring a profound sense of peace and acceptance, even in the face of our deepest struggles.

Another important aspect of understanding our inner divinity is self-compassion. It is easy to be harsh and critical of ourselves, especially when we are suffering. However, embracing a compassionate attitude towards ourselves can be transformative. It allows us to see our pain through a lens of kindness and understanding, rather than judgment and blame. This shift in perspective can open the door to healing, as we learn to treat ourselves with the same care and respect that we would offer to a dear friend.

Moreover, acknowledging our inner divinity can inspire us to seek out and create connections with others.

When we recognize the divine within ourselves, we are more likely to see it in those around us. This can foster a sense of empathy and solidarity, as we come to understand that we are all on a shared journey of growth and discovery. By supporting and uplifting each other, we can create a community of healing and resilience.

Ultimately, understanding the divinity within is about embracing our true selves. It is about recognizing that, despite our struggles, we are inherently worthy and capable of transcending our challenges. This awareness can provide a foundation of strength and hope, enabling us to navigate the complexities of grief, anxiety, and depression with greater clarity and purpose. In this way, we can transform our suffering into a source of profound personal and spiritual growth.

Chapter 12: Finding the Way Within

The Door Within

When the world seems to stand still, there exists a space within us, a threshold to an inner realm where emotions are not just felt, but explored and understood. This space is not physical; it is a mental and emotional passage, a door that leads to the depths of our being. It is here, in this sanctuary of introspection, that we encounter our grief, anxiety, and depression.

Grief, is a visitor - unacquainted and uninvited and arrives unannounced, carrying the weight of loss and the echoes of memories. It is a complex visitor, weaving through the corridors of our mind, touching upon moments of joy now tinged with sorrow. As we stand before this door, we are invited to reflect on the nature of our loss, to acknowledge the pain, and to honor the significance of what once was. Grief asks us to sit with it, to allow its presence without rushing to banish it. In this acceptance, we begin to understand that grief is not an enemy but a testament to love and connection.

Anxiety soon follows, often more insidious in its approach. It slips through the cracks of our consciousness, manifesting as a restless energy, a constant hum of unease. It thrives on uncertainty and the unknown, feeding on our fears and doubts. As we venture deeper into this inner landscape, we are confronted with the myriad ways anxiety shapes our thoughts and behaviors. It is a relentless companion, urging us to anticipate the worst, to prepare for every possible outcome. Yet, in acknowledging its presence, we find the opportunity to challenge its hold, to question its validity, and to seek out the calm within the storm.

Depression, the third and perhaps most formidable presence, is a shadow that envelops us, dimming the light of hope and joy. It is a heavy, pervasive force that saps our energy and colors our world in shades of gray. Within this inner space, depression demands our attention, urging us to recognize the depth of our despair. It is a call to introspection, to explore the root causes of our sadness and to confront the feelings of worthlessness and hopelessness that it brings. By facing depression head-on, we can begin to dismantle its grip, piece by piece, and seek out the glimmers of light that persist even in the darkest times.

This journey through the door within is not a linear path; it is a winding, often tumultuous exploration of our innermost selves. It requires patience, courage, and a willingness to embrace vulnerability. In this space, we learn that our emotions, no matter how overwhelming, are an integral part of our human experience. They are not to be feared or suppressed, but understood and integrated.

As we navigate this inner realm, we come to realize that the door within is not just an entryway to our pain, but also a passage to healing and growth. It is a reminder that we possess the strength to face our deepest fears and the capacity to emerge from the darkness with a renewed sense of self. In this reflective space, we find not only the weight of our struggles but also the resilience of our spirit.

Connecting with the Source

The experience of grief, anxiety, and depression often feels like a solitary endeavor, a dark tunnel where the light at the end seems perpetually out of reach. Yet, within this darkness, there lies an opportunity to connect with a deeper source of strength and understanding. This connection, though not always evident, becomes a lifeline, a beacon guiding us through the shadows.

In moments of profound sorrow or overwhelming anxiety, we may find ourselves questioning the very fabric of our existence. The weight of our emotions can obscure our sense of purpose, leaving us adrift in a sea of uncertainty. It is precisely in these moments that turning inward to connect with the source of our pain can also reveal the source of our healing.

This source is multifaceted, encompassing our inner resilience, our capacity for empathy, and our inherent need for connection. It is a place where we are allowed to be vulnerable, where our true selves can emerge without fear of judgment. By acknowledging our pain and allowing ourselves to fully experience it, we open the door to a deeper understanding of our emotional landscape.

One way to connect with this source is through the practice of mindfulness. Mindfulness encourages us to be present with our emotions, to observe them without attachment or aversion. It teaches us to sit with our discomfort, to breathe through our anxiety, and to honor our grief. In doing so, we begin to cultivate a sense of inner peace, a quiet strength that sustains us even in our darkest hours.

Another path to this source is through the act of self-compassion. Often, we are our harshest critics, berating ourselves for feeling weak or inadequate. Self-compassion invites us to treat ourselves with the same kindness and understanding that we would offer a dear friend. It reminds us that our pain is not a sign of failure, but a testament to our humanity. By being gentle with ourselves, we create a space where healing can take root.

Connecting with others who have shared similar experiences can also be profoundly healing. Whether through support groups, therapy, or simply confiding in a trusted friend, sharing our stories allows us to feel less isolated. It reminds us that we are not alone in our struggles, that our pain is both unique and universal. In these connections, we find solace and strength, a reminder that we are part of a larger tapestry of human experience.

Spiritual practices, whether rooted in religion or personal belief systems, offer another avenue for connection. Prayer, meditation, and rituals can provide a sense of grounding, a way to connect with something greater than ourselves. These practices can offer comfort and a sense of purpose, helping us to navigate the complexities of our emotions with grace and resilience.

Ultimately, connecting with the source is about finding the threads of light within the darkness. It is about recognizing that even in our most difficult moments, there is a part of us that remains whole and unbroken. By nurturing this connection, we begin to reclaim our sense of self, to rediscover our capacity for joy and hope. It is a journey of transformation, one that leads us back to the heart of who we are.

Answers to Our Questions

When we are engulfed in the throes of grief, anxiety, and depression, our minds naturally seek answers. Why did this happen? Will I ever feel better? What steps should I take to heal? These questions, often whispered in the quietest moments of despair, are not just cries for understanding but also for a sense of control over the chaos within.

In the midst of emotional turmoil, clarity can seem elusive. Each individual's experience is unique, shaped by personal history, temperament, and circumstances. Yet, there are common threads that bind us in our search for resolution and peace.

The first step in finding answers often lies in acknowledging the complexity of our emotions. Grief, anxiety, and depression are not linear processes; they ebb and flow, sometimes intensifying without warning. Understanding this can prevent the frustration that comes with expecting a straightforward path to recovery. Accepting the unpredictable nature of these emotions allows us to be more compassionate with ourselves, recognizing that setbacks do not signify failure but are part of the healing process.

Another crucial aspect is the realization that seeking help is not a sign of weakness but an act of strength. Professional guidance, whether through therapy, counseling, or support groups, can provide invaluable insights and coping mechanisms. These resources offer a safe space to explore our feelings, gain perspective, and develop strategies to manage our mental health. They remind us that we are not alone, and that others have navigated similar struggles and emerged resilient.

Moreover, the importance of self-care cannot be overstated. Simple practices, such as maintaining a routine, engaging in physical activity, and prioritizing rest, can have profound effects on our well-being. These small acts of kindness towards ourselves help to ground us, offering stability in moments of emotional turbulence. It is through these daily rituals that we can begin to rebuild our strength and resilience.

Connection with others also plays a pivotal role in our journey towards answers. Sharing our experiences with trusted friends or family members can alleviate the burden of isolation. Their support, even when they cannot fully understand our pain, can provide comfort and validation. In these connections, we find reminders of our worth and the enduring bonds that can sustain us through difficult times.

Reflecting on our thoughts and feelings through journaling or creative expression can also be enlightening. These practices allow us to externalize our internal struggles, giving form to the formless and making the intangible tangible. Through this process, we often uncover insights and patterns that might otherwise remain hidden, guiding us towards a deeper understanding of ourselves and our emotions.

Answers to our questions may not always come in the form of definitive solutions but rather through an evolving process of self-discovery and growth. It is through patience, self-compassion, and the willingness to seek support that we gradually piece together the fragments of our broken hearts and minds.

In these moments of introspection and action, we begin to see glimmers of hope. The path may be fraught with challenges, but each step forward, no matter how small, is a testament to our strength and resilience. It is through this journey that we find not just answers, but also a renewed sense of purpose and the possibility of joy amidst the pain.

Reasons for Our Journey

The whispers of our hearts often lead us to places we never imagined we'd go. When faced with the overwhelming tides of grief, anxiety, and depression, we find ourselves navigating a labyrinth of emotions, seeking not just an escape, but understanding. It is within this search that we uncover the profound reasons that propel us forward.

Grief, in its rawest form, can shatter the very foundation of our existence. The loss of a loved one, a dream, or even a sense of self can leave us feeling untethered. Yet, within this devastation lies a compelling drive to find meaning amidst the chaos. We are urged to honor the memories, to keep alive the essence of what was lost. This deep-seated need to remember and cherish becomes a beacon, guiding us through the darkest nights.

Anxiety, with its relentless grip, often feels like an uninvited guest overstaying its welcome. It whispers fears and doubts, casting shadows over our every step. Yet, it also serves as a reminder of our vulnerability and our innate desire for safety and peace. This quest for tranquility pushes us to confront our fears, to seek solace in understanding and connection. The relentless pursuit of calm amidst the storm becomes an act of defiance, a testament to our resilience.

Depression, the silent thief of joy, can make even the simplest of tasks feel insurmountable. It casts a pall over our days, draining the color from our world. However, within its depths, there lies a profound yearning for light, for moments of genuine happiness. This intrinsic longing propels us to seek help, to reach out, and to find fragments of hope. It is this hope, however faint, that fuels our determination to reclaim our lives from the shadows.

Throughout our struggles, the human spirit reveals its remarkable capacity for growth and transformation. Each step we take is driven by an innate desire to heal, to find balance, and to rediscover our purpose. The act of seeking therapy, confiding in loved ones, or even turning to creative outlets becomes a testament to our will to survive and thrive. It is through these actions that we begin to stitch together the fragments of our shattered selves.

Our journey is not just a personal endeavor but a collective experience. The stories of others who have walked similar paths serve as both a mirror and a guide. Their tales of resilience and recovery remind us that we are not alone, that our struggles are shared, and that there is strength in solidarity. This sense of community provides a foundation upon which we can rebuild, offering support and understanding in times of need.

In the end, it is our unwavering desire for healing that propels us forward. The need to find peace within ourselves, to reconcile with our past, and to forge a future filled with purpose and joy drives us to confront our deepest fears and sorrows. It is this relentless pursuit of understanding and healing that defines our journey, illuminating the path ahead with the promise of brighter days.

Chapter 13: Taking the First Step

Making the Choice

Reflecting on the moments when the weight of grief, anxiety, and depression began to press heavily upon my shoulders, I am reminded of the profound complexity that accompanies the decision to seek help. It is often not a single, clear moment but a series of subtle, sometimes imperceptible shifts that gradually accumulate until the need for change becomes undeniable. The choice to confront these overwhelming emotions can feel like standing at the edge of an abyss, peering into a darkness that threatens to consume.

In those early days, the signs were often masked by the busyness of life. The persistent ache of loss, the gnawing worry that never seemed to fade, and the pervasive sense of hopelessness all intermingled with daily routines. Yet, there were moments of clarity, fleeting but powerful, where the realization struck that this was more than just a passing phase. It was during these moments that the internal dialogue began—a conversation filled with doubt, fear, and a flicker of hope.

The decision to seek help is deeply personal, often influenced by several factors. For some, it is the gentle urging of a loved one who sees the pain that has become invisible to oneself. For others, it is a moment of crisis where the only options seem to be to seek help or to continue down a path that feels increasingly untenable. The stigma surrounding mental health can add another layer of complexity, making the choice even more fraught with uncertainty.

There is a certain vulnerability in admitting that one cannot navigate these situations s alone. It requires a surrendering of pride, an acknowledgment of limitations, and a leap of faith into the unknown. The fear of judgment, both from oneself and others, can be paralyzing. Yet, within this vulnerability lies the potential for profound transformation. It is in the act of reaching out, of admitting that help is needed, that the first steps toward healing can begin.

Reflecting on my own journey, I recall the myriad of emotions that accompanied this decision. There was fear, yes, but also a deep-seated relief at the prospect of no longer having to carry the burden alone. The process of finding the right support—whether through therapy, medication, or other means—was not without its challenges. It required patience, persistence, and a willingness to try different approaches until the right fit was found.

The path to making this choice is rarely linear. It is often marked by setbacks and moments of doubt. However, each step taken, no matter how small, is a testament to the strength and resilience that lies within. The decision to seek help is not a sign of weakness, but rather an act of profound courage.

When reflecting on this pivotal moment, what stands out is the realization that the choice to seek help is not just a single decision, but a series of choices made each day. It is a commitment to oneself, a recognition of the value of one's own well-being, and a step towards reclaiming a sense of hope and possibility. Through this lens, the act of seeking help becomes not just a response to suffering, but a powerful affirmation of life and the potential for healing.

Willingness to Get Closer

In the depths of our emotional struggles, there exists a subtle yet profound shift that can begin to change everything: the decision to lean in rather than pull away. When faced with grief, anxiety, or depression, the instinctive reaction often is to create distance, to shield oneself from the overwhelming pain. Yet, it is in the willingness to get closer to these emotions that a path to healing can be found.

This willingness is not about diving headfirst into the abyss but rather about approaching our feelings with curiosity and compassion. It requires a gentle, mindful engagement with our inner world, acknowledging the hurt without the need to fix it immediately. The act of getting closer is an invitation to sit with our discomfort, to observe it, and to understand its nuances. In doing so, we begin to dismantle the barriers that keep us isolated from our own experiences and, consequently, from others.

A significant aspect of this process is recognizing the narratives we tell ourselves about our pain. Often, these stories are laden with judgment and fear, amplifying our suffering. By approaching our emotions with a willingness to listen and understand, we can start to rewrite these narratives. This shift in perspective allows us to see our struggles not as insurmountable obstacles but as parts of our human experience that deserve attention and care.

In the realm of grief, this might involve acknowledging the depth of our loss and giving ourselves permission to mourn fully. It's about allowing the tears to flow, the memories to surface, and the heartache to be felt. This openness can create a space where healing begins, not through the erasure of pain but through its integration into the fabric of our lives.

When it comes to anxiety, getting closer means facing our fears with a compassionate lens. It involves exploring the sources of our anxiety, understanding the triggers, and gently challenging the thoughts that perpetuate it. This approach can slowly diminish the power of anxiety over our lives, as we learn to coexist with it rather than be dominated by it.

Depression, with its heavy fog, often convinces us of our unworthiness and the futility of hope. Here, the willingness to get closer might look like reaching out for support, even when it feels impossible. It's about speaking our truth, no matter how bleak, and allowing others to hold some of that weight with us. In the light of shared humanity, the isolation of depression can begin to lift, revealing the possibility of connection and support.

This practice of getting closer also extends to our relationships. By being present with our own emotions, we cultivate the capacity to be present with others in their struggles. We become better listeners, more empathetic companions, and more attuned to the silent cries for help that often go unnoticed. This mutual vulnerability fosters deeper connections, weaving a safety net of understanding and support.

Ultimately, the willingness to get closer is an act of courage. It is the bravery to face our inner turmoil and the strength to seek understanding rather than escape. This process is neither quick nor easy, but it holds the promise of transformation. By approaching our grief, anxiety, and depression with an open heart, we can find a way through the darkness, not by avoiding it, but by walking through it with a renewed sense of compassion and self-awareness.

Start of the Journey

Setting out on the path to healing often feels like navigating through an unfamiliar landscape. The initial steps are hesitant, filled with uncertainty and a blend of hope and fear. This is a crucial phase where the weight of grief, anxiety, and depression can seem most overwhelming, yet it is also the beginning of understanding and transformation.

It starts with acknowledging the presence of these emotions, which is per se a brave . Denial is a common response to emotional pain. It is a protective mechanism that temporarily shields us from the full impact of our feelings. However, moving beyond denial is necessary for any real progress. It's about gently lifting the veil and allowing oneself to confront the reality of the situation. This confrontation is not about wallowing in sorrow but about recognizing the depth of one's emotions and the need for healing.

The next step involves seeking support. For some, it may be turning to friends and family, those who offer a listening ear and a comforting presence. For others, professional help from therapists or counselors provides a structured and safe environment to explore these feelings. It's important to remember that seeking help is not a sign of weakness but rather an act of strength and self-care. It is about building a support system that can provide stability and understanding during these trying times.

Another critical aspect is self-reflection. This involves looking inward and understanding how these emotions have affected one's life. Journaling can be a powerful tool in this process, allowing thoughts and feelings to be expressed freely without judgment. Writing about experiences and emotions can bring clarity and insight, helping to identify patterns and triggers that contribute to one's emotional state. It is through this self-awareness that one can begin to find ways to cope and manage these feelings more effectively.

In addition, engaging in activities that promote mental and physical well-being plays a significant role in this phase. Exercise, meditation, and creative pursuits like art or music can provide a much-needed outlet for pent-up emotions. These activities help in releasing stress and fostering a sense of achievement and joy, even if momentary. They serve as reminders that life, despite its challenges, still holds moments of beauty and pleasure.

Understanding that progress is not linear is also essential. There will be days that feel like steps backward, where emotions surge and the pain feels as fresh as ever. These moments are part of the process and should not be viewed as failures. Each individual's journey is unique, and comparing oneself to others can lead to unnecessary frustration and self-doubt. Patience and compassion towards oneself are crucial during these times.

As one moves forward, the initial trepidation slowly gives way to a sense of resilience. Small victories, such as getting through a day with fewer tears or managing to find joy in a simple activity, are signs of progress. These moments, however fleeting, are indicators that healing is taking place. They provide the motivation to continue, to keep pushing through the darkness towards a place of light and peace.

In this phase, the first steps are tentative and fraught with challenges, but they are also filled with the promise of growth and healing. It is a journey that requires courage, support, and a deep well of self-compassion. With each step, the path becomes a little clearer, the burden weighs a little lighter , and the heart a little stronger. .

Accomplishing Goals

Navigating through grief, anxiety, and depression often feels like an insurmountable task. Yet, within this emotional tempest, there exists an anchor—a sense of purpose that can guide us towards stability and healing. Setting and accomplishing goals becomes a vital aspect of this journey, providing both direction and a sense of achievement, even in the smallest of victories.

Often, the weight of our emotions can cloud our vision, making it difficult to see beyond the immediate pain. It is in these moments that setting realistic and manageable goals can offer a semblance of control. The goals need not be grand; in fact, smaller, more attainable objectives can be profoundly impactful. Simple tasks such as making the bed each morning or taking a short walk can serve as stepping stones towards larger aspirations.

One of the first steps in this process is to acknowledge where we are emotionally and mentally. Understanding our current state allows us to set goals that are both realistic and compassionate. This self-awareness is not always easy to achieve, especially when grief and anxiety cloud our judgment. However, by taking the time to reflect on our feelings and capabilities, we can identify goals that are within our reach.

Creating a plan is essential. This plan should be flexible, allowing for adjustments as needed. Life is unpredictable, and so are our emotional states. By permitting ourselves the grace to adapt our goals, we can avoid the trap of self-criticism when things do not go as planned. This flexibility is not a sign of weakness but rather a testament to our resilience and understanding of the complexities of our emotional landscape.

It is important to celebrate small victories. Each step forward, no matter how insignificant it may seem, is a testament to our strength and determination. These moments of success can serve as reminders of our capability, providing a counterbalance to the often-overwhelming feelings of helplessness. Keeping a journal to document these achievements can be a powerful tool, offering a tangible record of progress that can be revisited during more challenging times.

Support systems play a crucial role in achieving our goals. Whether it is friends, family, or professional counselors, having someone to lean on can make a significant difference. These individuals can offer encouragement, provide perspective, and help us stay accountable. They can also remind us that we are not alone in our struggles, which is a comforting thought when the weight of our emotions feels too heavy to bear alone.

Self-compassion is another critical element. It is easy to fall into the trap of self-criticism, especially when progress feels slow or non-existent. However, it is essential to treat ourselves with the same kindness and understanding that we would offer a dear friend. Recognizing that healing is a process which has to be worked upon in one's own time and space, allows us to be more forgiving of ourselves.

In the middle of grief, anxiety, and depression, accomplishing goals might seem like an uphill task. Yet, by setting realistic objectives, creating flexible plans, celebrating small victories, relying on support systems, and practicing self-compassion, we can navigate this challenging terrain. Each goal achieved, no matter how small, is a beacon of hope, illuminating the path towards healing and resilience.

Chapter 14: Becoming a Channel

Role of a Channel

In the labyrinth of human emotions, grief, anxiety, and depression often intertwine, creating a complex tapestry that can be difficult to navigate. These emotions, though distinct, share common threads that bind them together in the human experience. They are not just states of mind but deeply rooted responses to life's challenges and losses. The role of a channel in this context becomes crucial, serving as a conduit through which these emotions can be expressed, understood, and ultimately transformed.

A channel can take many forms. It might be any person who offers a listening ear and an empathetic heart or it could be an activity, like writing, painting, or playing music, that allows for the release of pent-up feelings. The essence of a channel lies in its capacity to facilitate the flow of emotions, providing a safe space for their expression and exploration.

For those grappling with grief, a channel can help in acknowledging and honoring the loss. Grief is a natural response to losing someone or something significant, and it encompasses a range of emotions from sadness to anger to guilt. These feelings can be overwhelming and isolating, but when they are given an outlet, they become somewhat manageable. A channel can offer the opportunity to share memories, express sorrow, and find solace during pain. It allows the grieving process to unfold naturally, without the pressure to 'move on' or 'get over it'.

Anxiety, on the other hand, is often rooted in fear and uncertainty. It manifests as a constant state of worry, restlessness, and a sense of impending doom. A channel for anxiety provides a way to externalize these fears, giving them a form and a voice. This can be through journaling, where one can articulate their worries and examine them more objectively, or through physical activities like yoga and exercise, which help to release the tension held within the body. By channeling anxiety into constructive outlets, it becomes possible to reduce its grip and regain a sense of control.

Depression, characterized by persistent feelings of sadness, hopelessness, and a lack of interest in life, can be particularly challenging to navigate. The role of a channel in this context is to offer a lifeline, a way to break through the numbness and reconnect with the self and the world. This might involve engaging in creative pursuits that bring joy and satisfaction, or seeking out social connections that provide support and understanding. A channel can also include professional help, such as therapy or medication, which can offer the tools needed to manage and alleviate depressive symptoms.

In all these cases, the role of a channel is not to eliminate grief, anxiety, or depression, but to provide a means to cope with and process these emotions. It is about finding ways to live with them, to understand their origins and impacts, and to integrate them into the broader narrative of one's life. By doing so, it becomes possible to move forward with greater resilience and self-awareness.

Reflecting on the role of a channel in dealing with grief, anxiety, and depression highlights the importance of not facing these emotions alone. It underscores the value of connection, expression, and self-care in navigating the turbulent waters of human emotion. Through the use of channels, one can find pathways to healing and growth, transforming pain into a source of strength and insight.

Enabling Others

Supporting others through their struggles with grief, anxiety, and depression often requires a delicate balance of empathy, understanding, and gentle encouragement. This chapter delves into the profound impact one can have by simply being present and offering a compassionate ear. It's about recognizing the power of small, consistent actions and words that can help someone feel less isolated and more understood.

When someone close to us is grappling with emotional pain, the instinct to fix their problems can be strong. However, it's crucial to remember that our role is not to solve their issues but to provide a safe space where they can express their feelings without fear of judgment. Listening actively, without the urge to interject with solutions, validates their experience and reinforces that their emotions are important and worth acknowledging.

Creating an environment of trust is essential. This involves being reliable and consistent, showing up when promised, and maintaining confidentiality. Trust is the foundation upon which individuals feel secure enough to open up about their deepest struggles. It's in these moments of vulnerability that true connection and healing can begin.

Offering practical support can also be immensely beneficial. Simple acts like helping with daily tasks, providing meals, or accompanying them to appointments can alleviate some of the burdens they face. These gestures demonstrate care and solidarity, showing that they are not alone in their journey. It's about being an anchor in their storm, offering stability when everything else seems uncertain.

Encouraging professional help is another vital aspect. While friends and family can offer tremendous support, mental health professionals possess the tools and expertise to guide someone through their healing process effectively. Gently suggesting therapy or counseling can be a pivotal step in their recovery. It's important to approach this suggestion with sensitivity, ensuring it comes from a place of concern and not judgment.

Education plays a significant role in enabling others. Understanding the nuances of grief, anxiety, and depression can help in providing better support. This might involve reading up on these conditions or attending support groups to gain insights. Knowledge equips us to recognize warning signs and respond appropriately, making us better allies in their struggle.

Patience cannot be overstated. Healing from emotional pain is rarely a linear process; it is filled with ups and downs, progress, and setbacks. Being patient means allowing them to move at their own pace, celebrating small victories, and offering encouragement when they falter. It's about being a steady presence, offering hope and reassurance even when the path seems long and arduous.

Self-care is equally important for those offering support. It's easy to become overwhelmed and emotionally drained when immersed in someone else's pain. Taking time to recharge, seeking support for oneself, and setting healthy boundaries ensures that we can continue to be effective and compassionate in our role.

Ultimately, enabling others through their grief, anxiety, and depression is about fostering a connection based on empathy, respect, and unwavering support. It's about walking alongside them, offering a hand to hold, and reminding them that they are not alone. Through our actions and words, we can provide help and hope to illuminate the path towards healing and recovery.

Moving Towards the Same

The path through the tangled woods of grief, anxiety, and depression often feels isolating, as if each step is taken in solitude. Yet, within this seemingly solitary trek, there lies a profound paradox: the more we delve into these emotional landscapes, the more we uncover common ground with others who are on their own journeys. The shared human experience of pain and recovery weaves an invisible thread that binds us together, even when we feel most alone.

It is a strange comfort to discover that our personal struggles are mirrored in the lives of others. This realization can be both humbling and empowering. When we acknowledge that our suffering is not unique, we begin to see that the emotions we wrestle with, are part of a larger human narrative. This shared narrative offers us a sense of belonging, a reminder that we are not outliers in our pain but part of a collective experience.

In the middle of our darkest moments, the stories of others can act as beacons of hope. Hearing about someone else's journey through grief or their battle with anxiety can provide a lifeline, a whisper that says, "You are not alone." These stories remind us that there is a way through the darkness, even if the path is not immediately visible. By connecting with others who have faced similar challenges, we begin to see that our own struggles are not insurmountable.

However, finding this common ground requires a willingness to be vulnerable. It means opening up about our pain and allowing others to share theirs. This openness can be daunting, as it exposes those parts of ourselves that we often wish to keep hidden. Yet, it is in this vulnerability that true connection is forged. When we share our stories, we invite others to do the same, creating a space where mutual understanding and support can flourish. .

The process of moving towards the same emotional space as others also involves a shift in perspective. Instead of viewing our pain as an isolated incident, we start to see it as part of the broader human condition. This shift can be transformative. It encourages us to look beyond our own suffering and consider the experiences of those around us. In doing so, we cultivate empathy and compassion, both for ourselves and for others.

Moreover, this shared understanding can lead to collective healing. When we come together to support one another, we create a community that is resilient and nurturing. This community becomes a source of strength, offering comfort and solace in times of need. It is within this supportive network that we find the courage to face our fears and the resilience to overcome our challenges.

The journey through grief, anxiety, and depression is undoubtedly arduous, but it is made more bearable by the connections we forge along the way. By recognizing the common threads in our experiences, we move towards a place of mutual understanding and support. This movement towards the same is not a destination but an ongoing process, one that requires patience, empathy, and the willingness to be vulnerable. In embracing this process, we find that our individual struggles are part of a larger tapestry of human experience, one that is rich with shared meaning and collective strength.

Helping with Pain

Pain is an intricate part of the human experience, often manifesting in both physical and emotional forms. It is a universal language that binds us together, yet it can feel incredibly isolating. In the throes of grief, anxiety, and depression, pain can become an all-encompassing presence, making it difficult to see beyond the immediate suffering. However, helping others with their pain—whether it is through acts of kindness, empathetic listening, or simply being present—can be profoundly healing for both the giver and the receiver.

When we encounter someone in pain, our first instinct may be to offer solutions or advice. While these gestures come from a place of genuine concern, they can sometimes feel dismissive to the person suffering. What many people in pain truly need is to feel heard and understood. Active listening, where we give our full attention without interrupting or judging, can provide immense comfort. It validates the person's feelings and shows them that they are not alone in their struggle.

Empathy is another crucial element in helping with pain. It involves putting ourselves in another person's shoes and experiencing their emotions as if they were our own. This deep connection fosters a sense of solidarity and can alleviate feelings of isolation. Simple expressions like, "I can't imagine what you're going through, but I'm here for you," can go a long way in providing emotional support.

Physical presence also plays a significant role. Sometimes, words are not enough, and our presence becomes the most powerful form of support. Sitting in silence with someone, holding their hand, or offering a comforting hug can convey a depth of care that words often cannot. These small acts of solidarity can be a lifeline for someone drowning in pain.

It's important to recognize that helping with pain is not about fixing the problem but about being there through the highs and lows. Pain is a complex, multifaceted experience that cannot always be resolved quickly or easily. Offering ongoing support, checking in regularly, and being patient are essential aspects of providing meaningful help.

Self-care is equally important for those who support others in pain. Bearing witness to another's suffering can be emotionally draining, and it is crucial to replenish our own emotional reserves. Engaging in activities that bring joy, seeking support from others, and setting healthy boundaries can help maintain our well-being while we support others.

Sometimes, professional help may be necessary. Encouraging someone to seek therapy or counseling can be a vital step in their healing process. Mental health professionals are equipped with the tools and expertise to guide individuals through their pain and help them develop coping strategies.

In the end, helping with pain is about creating a space where people feel safe to express their emotions and get closer to the realization that they are not alone. It's about showing up, listening, and offering our presence without judgment or the need to fix. Through these acts of compassion, we can help alleviate some of the burden of pain and foster a sense of connection and hope.

www.ingramcontent.com/pod-product-compliance
Lightning Source LLC
LaVergne TN
LVHW041843070526
838199LV00045BA/1418